Joanna Murray-Smith's plays have been produced throughout Australia and all over the world, including *Honour*, which had a public reading with Meryl Streep and was produced on Broadway in 1998, the National Theatre, London, in 2003, and on the West End with Dame Diana Rigg in 2005. Other plays include *Fury*; *Songs for Nobodies*; *Switzerland*; *Pennsylvania Avenue*; *True Minds*; *Day One, A Hotel, Evening*; *Rockabye*; *Ninety*; *Bombshells*; *Rapture*; *Nightfall*; *Redemption*; *Love Child*; *Atlanta*; *Flame* and acclaimed adaptations of *Hedda Gabler* and *Scenes from a Marriage*, many of which have been translated into other languages. She has been nominated for and won many awards. Her novels include *Truce* and *Judgement Rock*, both published by Penguin Australia, and *Sunnyside*, published by Penguin Australia and Viking in the UK.

From left: Kate Atkinson as Annie, Katherine Tonkin as Bonnie and Catherine McClements as Tess in the Melbourne Theatre Company 2017 production. (Photo: Jeff Busby)

THREE LITTLE WORDS

JOANNA MURRAY-SMITH

CURRENCY PRESS
The performing arts publisher

CURRENCY PLAYS

First published in 2019
by Currency Press Pty Ltd,
PO Box 2287, Strawberry Hills, NSW, 2012, Australia
enquiries@currency.com.au
www.currency.com.au

Typeset by Dean Nottle for Currency Press.
Printed by Fineline Print + Copy Services, St Peters, NSW.
Cover design by Alissa Dinallo for Currency Press.

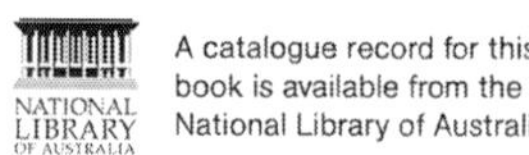

Contents

To Poli Papapetrou,
darling friend.

INTRODUCTION

'The world is a hellish place, and bad writing is destroying the quality of our suffering.'

Admittedly not a promising quote with which to begin the introduction to a new published work. This is actually a Tom Waits quote I keep above my desk. As a warning. And a challenge.

Joanna Murray-Smith has been elevating the quality of our suffering for over thirty years. Safe to say she has suffered in the service of doing it too. She lives and breathes her art. She doesn't just lose sleep over it, she forgoes it. She lives life fully immersed and shares its vicissitudes with us. Her body of work is formidable. She is truly a force of nature; prolific, probing and ever questing.

Strangely (considering we are both Melbourne-based writers) I first met Joanna at a New York Stage & Film Festival in the summer of 1996 in Upstate New York. Her masterpiece, *Honour*, was receiving a staged reading with some wannabe actress playing the title role. I forget her name. Meryl somebody… It'll come to me. I had seen the premiere production at Playbox (The Malthouse) in 1995 where I had that crushing/exhilarating theatre experience every playwright dreads/seeks when you come face to face with a written work that raises the bar at the same time as sending you into a self-loathing foetal position. It was a sublime piece of dramatic writing, the kind of work that makes you… Streep! Meryl Streep, that's it!

One of the quandaries of a writer's professional life is that working with a genuinely great actor is a double-edged sword. For they will both elevate and expose you. Especially in the bare bones crucible of a play reading. On the one hand, they make the text sound better than you ever dared dream. On the other, every flaw is laid utterly bare. Because, frankly, if they can't make it work then the writer has nowhere to hide. What struck me profoundly at the New York Stage & Film reading was that the writing not only held up under the white-hot scrutiny of a great actor, but it actually held Meryl Streep up. It supported her. The play is so immaculately written that it delivers its actors to rarefied air. Which is not to diminish the skill of actors, rather to celebrate the writer as architect of that truth and beauty.

Three Little Words is the kind of theatre that Joanna Murray-Smith specialises in: rocking our foundations by stealth. Using the Trojan Horse of whip-smart social comedy, she gains entry to our inner sanctum before confronting us with ideas that disrupt our default state of comfortable denial. I defy anyone in a long-term intimate relationship not to feel as if their secret fears and desires have been utterly unveiled. Because this is an author with a gimlet eye for the inner workings of heart, mind and spirit. Through her characters she articulates the suppressed doubts, dreads and yearnings residing deep in our core. Her gift is to dance in the shadows of who we really are. To remind us that an unexamined life is not worth living. Never didactic, always provocative and ambiguous, Joanna Murray-Smith delivers substance and existential heft in the most entertaining of packages. Because when she chooses to be she is flat-out razor-sharp funny. And this is a play that makes you laugh out loud often. On stage and on the page. It's sophisticated, top shelf comedy with genuine toe-curling bite.

One of the misconceptions about Joanna Murray-Smith's plays is that they are only concerned with the elite ruling class and reaffirm prevailing paradigms and social hierarchies. I disagree. They are, in fact, deft and deceptive provocations. Cattle prods to our inhibitions and fears. This is an unflinching playwright who creates incendiary characters who dare to turn their lives upside down. Who look the abyss dead in the eye. Who question their long-term marriage or propose giving up their only child. And not just in the heat of the moment but as a considered, angst-ridden decision. Joanna does what every great writer does: she writes what she knows then surprises herself and the audience with what she uncovers lurking beneath. William Shakespeare wrote deeply human plays about kings and queens. Joanna Murray-Smith writes deeply human plays about opinionated, erudite intellectuals, all arguing the toss, fighting for power and primacy in the battlefield of private and personal spaces. This was the world she grew up in. It's in her blood. And she mines it mercilessly, skewering shortcomings and hubris, in search of greater meaning.

Joanna Murray-Smith's plays have been staged all over the world. From large proscenium theatres on the Great White Way and the West End to little black boxes on the wrong side of town. Her words, ideas, characters, stories and the worlds she creates cast a potent spell wherever they go. They pulse and hum and teem with life. They elevate our suffering by offering insight and understanding about what it is to be human while shining a light into the dark recesses of our collective soul.

Matt Cameron
January 2019

Matt Cameron is an Australian playwright and screenwriter.

ACKNOWLEDGEMENTS

My thanks go to the passionately engaged Sarah Goodes and the brilliant first cast of *Three Little Words*, Catherine McClements, Katherine Tonkin, Kate Atkinson and Peter Houghton, for contributing so much to the play in the readings and rehearsal period. Thanks, as always, to all at the Melbourne Theatre Company, Currency Press and to Raymond Gill.

JM-S

Three Little Words was first produced by Melbourne Theatre Company at Southbank Theatre, The Sumner, on 18 April 2017 with the following cast:

ANNIE	Kate Atkinson
CURTIS	Peter Houghton
TESS	Catherine McClements
BONNIE	Katherine Tonkin

Director, Sarah Goodes
Set and Costume Designer, Michael Hankin
Lighting Designer, Paul Jackson
Composer and Sound Designer, Kelly Ryall
Assistant Director, Elsie Edgerton-Till
Fight Choreographer, Nigel Poulton
Tap Choreographer, Nathan Pinnell
Dramaturgy Consultant, Brent Hazelton
Stage Manager, Julia Smith
Assistant Stage Manager, Benjamin Cooper

CHARACTERS

BONNIE, mid 40s, strong

ANNIE, seven or eight years younger than Bonnie, pretty, fragile

TESS, mid 40s

CURTIS, mid 40s

SETTING

The design of the play should be able to accommodate a number of different settings in very swift transitions.

PROLOGUE

Evening. Curtis and Tess's stylishly raffish inner-city house.

As the audience enters, BONNIE *and* ANNIE*, a couple, are chatting (silent but animated) at the dining table with* CURTIS *and* TESS*, who are—metaphorically—their heterosexual twins.*

The detritus of a meal is on the table with empty bottles of wine.

As the lights dim, TESS *gets up from the group and walks to the front of the stage, as if looking out through a window. She looks, for a moment, almost other worldly and removed from the scene continuing behind her, her expression one of enigmatic curiosity and deep reflection.*

She turns her head and takes in the sight of CURTIS *at the table. He looks across at her for a tender moment of communion between them—a breakout from the scene at the table.*

TESS: Hey.

Beat.

CURTIS: Hey.

SCENE ONE

CURTIS, BONNIE *and* ANNIE *move over to the sofas, as if post-meal, carrying wine and glasses.*

TESS *joins them, now a part of the scene and mid-anecdote. The mood is infectiously good-humoured, tipsy and intimate.*

TESS: So … I picked up this rumpled copy of *Tender is the Night* and raced after him over the lawns and said: Excuse me! And he turned.

CURTIS: [*playing along*] Me?

TESS: I think you left this on the bench thing. He hesitated.

ANNIE: Thought bubble: Why is this incredibly beautiful woman calling out to me?

CURTIS: Oh God. Thank you! (She was ravishing. Even in that outfit.)

TESS: It was the era of those goat-wool ponchos. The ones the Flutes of the Andes guys wear when they're blowing whistles in shopping malls?

BONNIE: I absolutely cannot see you in a poncho, Tess.

CURTIS: She totally rocked a poncho.

TESS: He took the book and I said: It's kind of great, isn't it?

CURTIS: Isn't it? My God! What a writer!

TESS: What a writer, he said. The language, I said.

CURTIS: His fascination with the surfaces of privilege but his ability to plumb the ironic, tragic depths beneath—I guess you have a class now?

TESS: I guess you have a class now, he said.

CURTIS: She said no. Miracle.

TESS: We went to Genevieve's. I had a cappuccino. They were ninety-five cents. He had a Rage Against the Machine album.

CURTIS: She said she liked Alice in Chains.

TESS: I didn't really but I was trying to be cool.

CURTIS: I hated Alice in Chains. I told her that.

TESS: So I said: I don't know why I said that. I don't like them either. He thought I was an airhead.

CURTIS: You were beautiful and funny.

TESS: Walking home from Genevieve's, we passed a dog that had been hit by a car. And the driver was standing on the footpath crying and there were onlookers and everyone was comforting her but Curtis just sat down on the kerb and stroked the dog. He died with Curtis patting him.

CURTIS: [*not true, modest*] It was all an act.

TESS: Note to self: He cares.

CURTIS: Later, I was carrying on about saving rainforests and she suddenly started tap-dancing! Right there on the street!

TESS *does a fabulous little tap-dance. Cries of delight.*

Why are you tap-dancing?

TESS: [*dancing*] Whenever someone says 'rainforest', I tap.

CURTIS: Like that was normal!

TESS: It was a dare I lost. Had to tap on 'rainforest' for a year.

CURTIS: She keeps her word, I thought.

TESS: He looked like an artist. All wild hair and that little tattoo on his wrist: the Rolling Stones tongue. I hated tatts, even then, but there was something irresistible about a bad boy who loves Scott Fitzgerald. I'm in.

Laughter.

Cute noises from BONNIE *and* ANNIE, *touched by the romantic story. They kiss lightly but attentively. No self-consciousness.*

CURTIS *walks over to the bookshelf and pulls out a battered copy of* Tender is the Night.

CURTIS: And somewhere, some poor guy is wondering whatever happened to his copy of *Tender is the Night*.

Exclamations. Laughter. Convivial castigation.

TESS: What a phony!

BONNIE and ANNIE: [*simultaneously*] Total phony! / God, what a fake!

Beat.

TESS *and* CURTIS *look at each other, watched by* BONNIE *and* ANNIE. *A serious moment amidst the merriment.*

BONNIE *and* ANNIE *lift their glasses, recognising the unspoken.*

BONNIE: Congratulations you two.

ANNIE: Amazing feat.

They drink but neither TESS *nor* CURTIS *drink on cue.*

After a powerful moment of eye contact, CURTIS *raises his glass to* TESS. *They drink.*

I can't believe you weren't going to mark it!

BONNIE: Twenty years!

CURTIS: No, you're right. When we saw you at the installation thing with the meerkats, we re-evaluated. We said:

TESS: 'They're right.' [*Aside to* BONNIE] Great shoes.

BONNIE: [*aside to* TESS] Vintage Prada. Seventy bucks.

CURTIS: We have to give thanks for what we've had.

BONNIE: You bet you do.

ANNIE: Sometimes you know, just when Bonnie is folding the laundry or chopping carrots, I just say: Hey, babe, let's just stop and recognise that here we are, chopping carrots, folding laundry …

BONNIE: Stop or I'm going to cry!

ANNIE: I know it's kind of hokey …

TESS: Don't make fun of her, Bon. It's really true. We need to say these things: I love you. All of you.

ANNIE, BONNIE and CURTIS: [*simultaneously*] Oooh. / That's so lovely. / That's beautiful, babe. / Right back at ya …

TESS: Did Curtis tell you? Lola got a tattoo!

ANNIE and BONNIE: [*simultaneously*] No! / She did not!

TESS: You know how I feel about tattoos!

ANNIE: You hate tattoos!

TESS: I hate tattoos!

BONNIE: Is that even legal?

CURTIS: All the weapons in Cluedo. You know, the gun, the rope, the dagger—

TESS: Six, because her phone died so she couldn't Google the seventh.

CURTIS: We gave her hell! If you're going to rebel, do your research!

BONNIE: The dagger, the lead pipe, the wrench—

ANNIE: There's definitely another one!

BONNIE: When she worked for me that weekend of the art fair, she just kept saying: Bonnie, you are a genius. The implication being that I was pulling the wool over everyone's eyes.

TESS: How rude!

CURTIS: That's my girl!

BONNIE: I said: Lola, this artist is a profoundly interesting interpreter of this time and place.

ANNIE: Whatever, she said.

Laughter.

'Whatever'!

CURTIS: She's the patron saint of consumerism! Once upon a time you were dragged to church. You were delivered a meaning for existence. Now kids find it at Zara.

TESS: Thank God! Religion is the biggest terrorist of them all.

BONNIE: Amen.

CURTIS: Sticking with the red?

ANNIE: No more!

BONNIE: I'll have a Scotch if you've got it.

ANNIE: Really?

BONNIE *and* ANNIE *exchange a brief glance.*

As CURTIS *continues to speak he walks across to a shelf and pours the Scotch from a crystal decanter in a beautiful, antique tantalus.*

As he pours, BONNIE *notes it:*

BONNIE: That's fancy.

TESS: Grandpa's tantalus.

CURTIS: They used to lock them so the maid couldn't take a slug!

BONNIE: Hey, are you two going to Stig's dance-thingo?

CURTIS *catches* TESS*'s eye.*

CURTIS: Luckily, it's parent-teachers' night.

BONNIE: God, Curtis, I really wish you'd get out of teaching. You're underpaid and overqualified. Come over to the dark side.

CURTIS: Bonnie, I admire you for selling rich people high-concept shit to put on their walls but I'd rather see kids' faces light up when you read them *Madame Bovary*.

BONNIE: So you *do* read the classics?

CURTIS: I came around.

TESS: Every time we go out some kid says: Mr Miller, you were the best teacher ever.

ANNIE: Of course he is!

CURTIS: Once in a blue moon!

BONNIE: What's sexier than a bright student and a good-looking teacher?

TESS: You could be jailed for that!

BONNIE: Fantastic *tarte citron*.

TESS: Annie made me buy it. We saw that girl at the patisserie. That student, Curtis. The one who got expelled.

CURTIS: Who?

TESS: She was always running down everyone.

CURTIS: Oh, Greta something? The stream of consciousness reputation-slayer! Frida Kahlo— 'Overrated'! Wei Wei— 'Wish he'd go away-way'.

TESS: She's just made a short film. Wants us to come to a screening.

ANNIE: [*to* BONNIE, *waving a postcard*] She invited us, too.

CURTIS: Good for her. She was clever. A bit precocious, perhaps.

TESS: Great looking.

ANNIE: Amazing breasts.

BONNIE: You noticed?

ANNIE: Of course I noticed! My father was a cop—he was always prepping us in case we had to do an identikit.

TESS: She was pretty sexy!
CURTIS: She's a student, guys! Young women are constantly objectified, as you well know. I would have thought better of all three of you.
TESS: [*teenage voice*] Does this mean we get a detention, sir?

The three women giggle.

More Scotch!

CURTIS *pours. They all laugh.*

BONNIE: If you're having one.
ANNIE: [*to* BONNIE] Is that a good idea?
TESS: So listen.

Beat.

We're splitting.
BONNIE: [*going along with the joke*] You're splitting!
TESS: We are. We're breaking up.
ANNIE: Stop it!
BONNIE: Not funny! You're horrible!

From left: Peter Houghton as Curtis, Catherine McClements as Tess, Kate Atkinson as Annie and Katherine Tonkin as Bonnie in the Melbourne Theatre Company 2017 production. (Photo: Jeff Busby)

ANNIE: You're both horrible!

BONNIE: I hate you!

ANNIE: Not funny, you two.

Beat. BONNIE *looks at* TESS, *from her to* CURTIS.

BONNIE: What?

ANNIE: What?

BONNIE: What?

TESS *and* CURTIS *look at each other. Beat.*

CURTIS: It's a lot to take in.

TESS: Sorry. I mean, God!

CURTIS: As you can see, we are both okay. We really are. We are both okay about it. And if we're okay about it, you should be too.

ANNIE: [*to* TESS *and* CURTIS] Stop it! You're scaring me!

BONNIE: Not funny.

Beat.

Stop it!

ANNIE: What is this?

Beat.

What are you talking about?

CURTIS: We love you.

TESS: We'll always love you. It goes without saying. And we're still who we are.

Beat.

CURTIS: We're exactly who we were. Only we're who we were … split.

ANNIE: [*quietly*] You're breaking up?

BONNIE: No. No. Of course you're not.

ANNIE: What?

BONNIE: No, you're not.

TESS: Well—

BONNIE: You can't.

TESS *and* CURTIS *laugh ruefully.*

CURTIS: We were under the impression it was up to us.

Beat. ANNIE *and* BONNIE *look at each other for a second.*

BONNIE: You invited us to dinner to tell us you're splitting?

TESS: Yes.

ANNIE: [*dawning*] … It's your anniversary.

CURTIS *and* TESS *giggle.*

TESS: I know! It's crazy. But we got to twenty and that's nothing to scoff at.

ANNIE: But you are.

CURTIS: Oh, no—no!

TESS: Not at all.

ANNIE: What do you mean? You're splitting?

Beat.

What about Lola?

TESS: I agonised over the last year, paralysed with worry. But as it turns out, she's cool with it.

BONNIE: [*incredulous*] She's 'cool' with it?

CURTIS: She actually does seem to be cool with it. She wants her mother to be happy.

TESS: She's okay. She's really okay.

BONNIE *and* ANNIE *look at each other: Is this really happening?*

BONNIE: Is there … someone?

ANNIE: Is there someone else?

TESS and CURTIS: [*simultaneously*] No! / No, no, no!

CURTIS: There's no-one else.

TESS: There's no-one else.

BONNIE: There's no-one else?

TESS: There's no-one else. There's no-one else!

CURTIS: God, no.

Beat.

BONNIE: [*mystified*] So … sex?

CURTIS: Sex?

BONNIE: Is that the issue? Because after twenty—

TESS: God, no! No!

CURTIS: Never been our problem!

TESS: Still at it like a couple of bunnies.

ANNIE: 'A couple of bunnies'? But then why—?

TESS: *Sad* bunnies.

Beat. CURTIS *looks at* TESS. TESS *gives* CURTIS *silent permission.*

CURTIS: She's had enough.

BONNIE: Enough of … Curtis?

TESS: No. No. I love Curtis.

BONNIE: You love Curtis and he's a sexual dynamo but it's over? … I'm confused.

ANNIE: So it's not mutual?

CURTIS: If it were up to me … Listen, I don't know how I'm going to … but Tess has had enough—

BONNIE: [*to* TESS] What have you had enough of?

CURTIS: She has had enough of me.

TESS: No. No. Hey, Curtis, come on.

CURTIS: Well, maybe I'm loading that somewhat.

TESS: I love Curtis. I always will.

CURTIS: Ditto. Obviously. I adore her.

BONNIE: What the hell is wrong with you two?

CURTIS: I want her to feel she's the best version of herself. If our marriage can't help her find that version then I'm not going to impose any patriarchal pressure.

BONNIE: [*irritated*] What are you doing, Curtis?

CURTIS: I'm saying there are no bad guys here. It's about a primal need versus conventional security.

BONNIE: Why are you speaking for her?

TESS: Because he's a great guy.

BONNIE: So if he's such a great guy, why are you leaving him?

TESS: Because I—I— [*Struggling to find the words*] I suppose I need something …

CURTIS: She needs something, she's saying.

BONNIE: [*through gritted teeth*] I can hear her!

TESS: It's just a sense I have that—well—something's been forsaken.

BONNIE: Forsaken?

TESS: In marriage … We give something up to get something and now I wonder if what we lost wasn't quite important. We launch ourselves into roles—but but but then we forget—don't we? Or we never find out—what's there if we let those roles fall away?

BONNIE: [*changing tack, sweetly*] Tess—Tess—babe … Everyone has moments of doubt. It's natural. But it passes.

CURTIS: Maybe it shouldn't pass. Maybe the doubt is like a lantern guiding us towards something important.

BONNIE: Shut the fuck up, Curtis.

CURTIS: [*sotto voce*] Okay …

ANNIE: Now I just … God … I mean it's like I have to re-evaluate everything. I'm just—like—my mind is just spinning—

BONNIE: [*concerned*] Honey—

ANNIE: [*mystified, fraught*] Was that all a lie? Glamping? Tonga? When we went to the Kimberley? … When we sat up all night on New Year's and got smashed and danced in the rock pools. Were you just—was that—were you having us on?

CURTIS: We loved all those times!

TESS: We want more times like that!

BONNIE: What?

CURTIS: Separately—I mean—you know—

ANNIE: That's not going to work!

BONNIE: How would that work?

ANNIE: We're not going to Bhutan with one of you.

CURTIS: Why not? I want to come to Bhutan. Tess's not even all that into Bhutan.

BONNIE *looks at* TESS, *accusingly.*

BONNIE You wanted to go to Bhutan!

TESS: I wanted to make you happy! 'Cause I love you!

BONNIE: But I didn't want you to do us a favour. I wanted you to be as excited as we were!

TESS: I was excited *for* you! I can take or leave Bhutan.

CURTIS: Whereas I'm very into it.

ANNIE: We're not going to Bhutan with you, Curtis!

BONNIE: As if now, we could just go, the three of us, as if nothing had happened!

ANNIE: That's not going to work.

CURTIS: You're saying, 'It's four or nothing'?

BONNIE: Yes, I am!

CURTIS: I don't see why suddenly I'm out in the cold. I just bought *Time Out Bhutan*.

TESS: You're just shocked. You'll see—

CURTIS: Look, we might even both be able to come but just … as individuals. Instead of 'a unit'.

BONNIE: Fuck you!

ANNIE: Oh, as if! As if!

CURTIS: Why not?

BONNIE: [*suddenly furious*] Well, everything is 'twin share' for starters! It's going to be a lot more expensive with three rooms.

TESS: [*serious*] I could always have a roll-away in your room.

ANNIE: A roll-away!

BONNIE: Don't be stupid!

ANNIE: I don't want you on a roll-away!

BONNIE: Why are you doing this? You have a great marriage!

ANNIE: What started this?

Beat.

TESS: [*genuine, struggling*] It's a … yearning.

CURTIS: She says it's a yearning. I get that.

BONNIE: You seem to get everything.

ANNIE: [*affected by* TESS*'s words*] 'Yearnings'. That's a beautiful word.

BONNIE: Shit, Annie! What the fuck!

ANNIE: I'm just saying …

BONNIE: This whole thing is existential panic inspired by your mother.

ANNIE: You are so smart, babe!

TESS: [*lost in her own discovery*] You might be right, Bonnie. She was lying there, this woman I had known for forty-six years, whose hand had held mine for forty-six years. And she was dead and—suddenly it's me. On the frontline of mortality. Before long, I'm over. Forever. Can I have a drink please?

BONNIE *fills* TESS*'s glass.*

Seeing her body, lying there—I thought: I'm not a child anymore. I felt it. It's different for you—you don't have children. You've had the chance to really embrace your own ego. My entire identity has been child, wife, mother. And suddenly, the child was dead. And Lola is practically a woman. And I don't want to be defined as nothing more than a wife. Curtis's wife.

BONNIE: You're a very successful book editor.

TESS: I facilitate other people's creativity. What an epitaph! We're ciphers, Bonnie!

CURTIS: Ciphers.

BONNIE: [*affronted*] Well, I don't think that's exactly—

TESS: I want to be good to Curtis. Not to find his complaints about work pathetic. Not to hate the way he calculates tips on his phone or resent his inability to fantasise aloud. Love is not perfect. And so I have trained myself to forgive, to find excuses for his horrible traits, so that he in turn will judge me kindly. I want to be a good mother to Lola. I want to show kindness to strangers and give large amounts of money to orphans. But who notices? No-one! And sometimes I think that we need … to just occasionally be recognised as somehow … special …

BONNIE: Can't you be who you need to be with Curtis?

CURTIS: You can't reinvent yourself with the person who has been at your side for twenty-five years.

TESS: Their gaze … fixes you.

BONNIE: Isn't it comforting to be fixed?

ANNIE: When I met Bonnie, I was so happy that I could stop exploring and just settle into who she thought I was.

BONNIE: Tess, you come into the world already fully you. Other people just help you to discover who you already are.

TESS: That's a very constricting and uncreative way of seeing things. But even if it's true, Curtis sees me one way. And I see him one way as well.

BONNIE: And just throw it all away? The man who fathered your child, the years you shared, the growing up together?

CURTIS: She's not throwing it away, Bonnie.

TESS: [*still, resolved*] I'm putting it under a really beautiful glass dome. And I will look at it. And I will wonder at it. And I will be grateful for it. But I will not be defined by it.

CURTIS: Why should Tess be punished for wanting to know if there's anything better?

TESS: I've spent more of my life with Curtis than alone. We've become subsumed into a single entity. And it's a beautiful entity. And it made a beautiful child. But what if there's … nothing left of me? What if every last shred of *me* has been devoured by *us*?

CURTIS: You're so brave, Tessie.

TESS *and* CURTIS *smile at each other sweetly.*

BONNIE: [*to* CURTIS] What is wrong with you? Be a man, for Christ's sake!

CURTIS: It's the twenty-first century, Bonnie. This is what a man looks like.

BONNIE: Tess, you and Curtis will not be friends. You weren't friends before you hooked up! If Annie and I broke up, there is not a hope in hell that we would be friends.

ANNIE *looks confused by this.*

[*To* TESS *and* CURTIS] Do you realise how selfish you are? Do you realise the damage you do to other people when you give up? We have a duty. All of us. To stick it out.

ANNIE: … Or there'll be … an epidemic.

BONNIE: You'll start something.

ANNIE: If one of us gives up … it puts all of us in danger.

TESS: We're exactly who we've always been, guys.

ANNIE: 'Guys'! 'Guys'! How can you be so casual?!

BONNIE: You invite us here, into the house you have been inviting us to forever, part of our life together, our couple life, you invite us in here to eat lemon tart and you casually report that your world is imploding. Your world which is—effectively—*our* world. Your world which is our satellite and our world, which is your satellite which is supposed to keep on orbiting as if nothing has happened?

CURTIS: 'The couple life'?

ANNIE: Brilliant!

TESS: Did one small phrase ever summon more tedium? The acquisition of things, the throwing of dinner parties …

ANNIE: [*very upset*] I *like* the couple life. Okay? Okay? There's nothing wrong with it.

BONNIE: This is just … awful … You can't depend on something for years and then just abandon it—

CURTIS: She's not abandoning me—

ANNIE: We're not talking about you! We're talking about us.

BONNIE: We're family. Aren't we? We don't say hello when we call each other. We hang up without saying goodbye. And we loved you as one thing, not two.

TESS: That's the problem, Bonnie. The whole world sees us as one thing.

CURTIS: She needs to confirm she's something all by herself.

BONNIE: You really are quite the cheer squad.

TESS: And he does, too! There are a thousand other Curtises waiting to get out. This is for him, too.

ANNIE: Tess, this is a pretty scary undertaking.

TESS: Sure. But if I were you two, I'd be more terrified. Living with the thought that who you really are, alone in the truest sense, has been euthanased by the person you love most in the world?

ANNIE: I don't feel well.

BONNIE: *Euthanased?*

TESS: Yes, Bonnie, yes! The soundtrack to your couple life is the muffled cries of the dying individual as the pillow is held over the mouth! The birth of the couple can only happen at the hands of premeditated murder.

BONNIE: Fuck! What about Lola?

TESS: Life doesn't go as planned. Maybe we need to teach our children to be comfortable inside uncertainty.

ANNIE: That's a very powerful concept.

BONNIE: [*irritated*] Will you stop affirming her?

ANNIE: I'm just—

TESS: I'm getting rid of my mother's things. I don't want to be saddled with history. I'll give it all away and just buy Ikea because it's cheap and ubiquitous and doesn't touch your … soul. I'm quitting my job. I don't want to be in publishing. I'm tired of wrestling with things that aren't right or wrong. I don't want to do something that … hovers, like marriage. I don't want to do something vague and pointless and subjective like you and I do. I want to make the world better. I want to do something with a definable value.

Beat as BONNIE *looks at* TESS.

BONNIE: [*insulted*] Vague and pointless? I think that's a bit of a—

TESS: It's fine for you! But I want something deeper.

BONNIE: You realise you're in love with something that doesn't exist. There is no freedom. Freedom is like the Easter Bunny.

TESS: I know, that you two, in the darkest hour, have wondered—

ANNIE *is enthralled and frightened.* BONNIE *is dismissive.*

ANNIE and BONNIE: [*simultaneously*] Wondered?

TESS: What are you denying yourselves?

ANNIE: [*frightened*] Okay, okay, okay, okay—we have to go! We have to get out of here now!

ANNIE *gathers their things and ushers* BONNIE *towards the door.*

CURTIS *and* TESS *watch, curiously unruffled.*

When they get to the door ANNIE *and* BONNIE *stop suddenly, chillingly captivated by* TESS*'s words.*

TESS: Look into each other's eyes tonight and ask the question: Why are we here, night after night, day after day? When out there, so many possibilities lie in wait? Is it healthy to stick ourselves to another human in some kind of blind loyalty, even when, bit by bit, the energy dies? What is loyalty? It's the lie we tell ourselves to justify our fear.

SCENE TWO

One hour later. Bonnie and Annie's house.

ANNIE [*highly agitated*] He's been hijacked by her crazy ideas! When we did Pilates last week: not a peep!

BONNIE: Okay, at the installation thing—remember, I said: Dinner—it hasn't been just us for ages. And they said: Great, but come to ours.

ANNIE: No, it was Tess who suggested it. Tess said: What about coming over?—

BONNIE: Oh, that's right, she did.

ANNIE: And then you said: It's your anniversary so we should host—

BONNIE: I did say that.

ANNIE: And she said: No, no, no—we want to. Come to ours.

Beat.

BONNIE: They were already planning! Can you believe that?

ANNIE God!

BONNIE: But you know what, Annie? I'm not completely—

ANNIE: No?

BONNIE: Surprised, no.

ANNIE: Wow.

BONNIE: She's the person I love most, but Curtis is the deep one.

ANNIE: I've always loved Curtis.

BONNIE: I love Curtis.

ANNIE: I've loved Curtis since we were seventeen years old. When he and Tess first—well, you know. I thought she was a princess.

BONNIE: Who doesn't love Curtis? It broke my heart. God, he was so supportive and stoic!

ANNIE: He'll be leaning on us, Bon. Once it hits.

BONNIE: Even though I adore her, I've often thought she's never been all that warm.

ANNIE: Whenever I talk about my work, Tess sort of 'blanks out'. Like massage doesn't quite cut it in the world of big ideas.

BONNIE: Every so often, I think: God, you're actually quite cold.

ANNIE: She's one of those people who seems warm, but isn't. I love her but—

BONNIE: Right now it's hard not to love Curtis a little bit more. Yearnings!

ANNIE: And did you notice how much she drank?

BONNIE: Sure, but every female over forty is an alcoholic. I don't buy the sex being so great.

ANNIE: Really?

BONNIE: Can you see a naked Curtis whinnying around the bedroom?

ANNIE: Tess is always casually dropping that they have a lot of sex … Thrice weekly.

BONNIE: [*personally offended*] What?

ANNIE: That's what she said.

BONNIE: [*still reeling*] *Every* week? Doesn't leave much time for box sets! That's just bullshit. Obviously she was doing sexual 'public relations'. No-one does that. It's not even healthy.

ANNIE: I feel sick. I think I need to lie down.

BONNIE: Babe, lie down …

ANNIE: Why would anyone want to go back out there? Clubbing? Travelling solo? Going to parties all the time? Having to deal with sexual deviants on the dating scene?

BONNIE: [*realising how great*] Mmmmm.

ANNIE: Why would anyone want that?

BONNIE: They just landed us in the middle of their—failure. Just dumped us there. On a Friday night? After a big week. My God, how to wreck a nice evening!

ANNIE: That's just so insensitive.

BONNIE: Now I've booked Bhutan and no-one wants to go.

ANNIE: Curtis wants to go.

BONNIE: [*shocked*] I thought you were gung-ho?

ANNIE: I really want to want to go. It's just that I can't.

BONNIE: What does that mean?

ANNIE: It means I'm looking forward to being back from Bhutan and knowing I went.

BONNIE: We have to do something, Annie. You need to reach out to Curtis. He needs to feel part of the world again, be bolstered by youth and optimism. He needs to get back in the saddle.

ANNIE: Roger Wilco, Bonnie.

BONNIE: And I need to remind Tess—the grass is not greener. It's just a different green.

SCENE THREE

TESS *at home, lying on the couch, reading a magazine, drinking a vodka and uncharacteristically smoking a joint. Amy Winehouse: 'Rehab' on the radio. Euphorically alone.*

TESS *unconsciously starts singing along quietly. Slowly, she turns her attention to the song and turns the radio up. A little bit sozzled, she stands up and starts dancing her own eccentric, loose, whacky dance to the music, singing along.*

SCENE FOUR

The next day. ANNIE *and* CURTIS.

CURTIS *pacing, wound up, as* ANNIE *listens supportively.*

CURTIS: [*bottled up, spilling out*] Goddamnit, Annie. I thought I was okay! I really did. I mean … I didn't want this but I could see nothing was going to sway her. I thought it was going to be best for both of us if I got behind it. Was that pride? Or—or some misguided sense that reason prevails over emotions? What the fuck was I thinking? I was completely fucking deluded, Annie. I don't want this! This is crazy! We've been married for twenty years and okay sometimes we wanted to kill each other but we're as happy as anyone!

ANNIE Curtis …

CURTIS: I know I have to move out. I just can't bear the thought of it. I'll need someone with me when we're dividing stuff. Will you do it?

ANNIE: Of course I will.

He smiles wanly at her.

CURTIS: You're a great friend, Annie. I'm lucky to have you.

ANNIE: What you need is a youthful bolster.

CURTIS: One of those things for your back?

ANNIE: No … I'm saying you need to saddle up.

CURTIS: What does that mean?

ANNIE: I don't know. Bonnie said it. I think we're talking about someone to go to the movies with.

CURTIS: Annie, I've lost the love of my life. She's not replaceable.

ANNIE: You can't sit around feeling a failure.

CURTIS: Am I a failure, Annie? Maybe I just wasn't interesting enough.

ANNIE: You're one of the smartest people I know!

CURTIS: Smart's not the same as charismatic. Angela Merkel's smart.

ANNIE: Women look at you all the time. What about Ursula?

CURTIS: [*snorting with incredulity*] She's as old as the fucking hills, Annie!

ANNIE: She's your age.

CURTIS *is taken aback.*

You need someone who admires you. Someone who—I know! What about that gorgeous girl you used to teach that Tess and I met in the patisserie.

CURTIS: Annie! She's a kid!

ANNIE: [*no malice intended*] She looks up to you. That's not going come your way very often.

CURTIS: You're completely mad! My world has come crashing down! … I'm not one of those property developers who start wearing denim jackets and dating teens, Annie … that's just not me. Whatever I am, I'm not a fucking cliché! Annie … have you … have you and Bonnie—have you ever wondered?

ANNIE: [*very sensitive*] We don't wonder, Curtis! Okay!

CURTIS: I bet you have wondered.

ANNIE: Stop trying to make me catch something! Stop breathing on me. [*Calming down*] You weigh it up. All the time. Do you want love that builds mountains or love that moves mountains?

CURTIS: Hang on—so—which is better?

ANNIE: Obviously it's—well, okay, moving would be good too, but we've built a mountain. Building a mountain is not nothing, Curtis.

SCENE FIVE

BONNIE *and* TESS.

BONNIE: Let me explain what a mid-life crisis is. Two people make a good life together. After a while they get used to how good it is. Deep in their hearts they don't believe they deserve to be so happy. They start to sabotage that good life so that it starts to go wrong and they can reassure themselves that now they have the life they deserved to have. After a while, they get used to feeling vaguely unhappy and they start to get sick of it. So they convince themselves that they deserve something better having conveniently forgotten that they had something better before they fucked it up. Their boredom and discontent reaches the point where anything is better than what they have so they strap on an explosive vest and run into their happy house and blow it and themselves to smithereens. After the paramedics put them back together—and yes, Annie and I *are* paramedics—they go out there and start trying to make a new, better, life that is going to be spiritually nurturing and more evolved than the first one. They go out there full of hope and find that it's a barren landscape with a lot of battle-scarred middle-aged soldiers wandering around with brain injuries.

TESS: That was a very unpleasant homily, Bonnie, and actually rather tasteless.

BONNIE: [*annoyed and frustrated*] Oh alright, Tess! Alright! Have it your way! Saddle up! Go out there, back into the wilderness! Satisfy your yearnings! Explore the great unknown!

TESS: That's exactly what I plan to do, Bonnie.

BONNIE: I actually think if you go out there and see what's on offer, you're going to come screaming back. It's not pretty out there … But do it. Do it and see. [*Thinking*] You know, Tess … I actually think I might know someone.

TESS: You're going to set me up, Bonnie?

BONNIE: He's actually a very nice guy and fit. He cycles around Iceland every year. He's my accountant's brother.

TESS: I don't think so, Bonnie. I don't think I'm ready.

BONNIE: He drives a Tesla.

TESS: [*reconsidering*] That does sound promising. What does he do?

BONNIE: He's in I.T.

TESS: [*unequivocal*] Shit, no, Bonnie. No, Bonnie. I can't go that far.

BONNIE: This is my point, Tess. Everyone out there is in I.T. Or aged care. That's it. And I.T. is better than aged care. That's the entire dating scene for people your age. I want you to wake up to the fact that the paunchy entitled middle-aged man you've spent twenty years with who calculates tips on his phone is in all actuality a Greek god.

SCENE SIX

A theatre foyer. ANNIE *and* BONNIE *at interval.*

ANNIE: I like it but I don't understand anything.

BONNIE: You're not supposed to understand contemporary dance. It's whatever you want it to be.

ANNIE: But it's called 'Birth'.

BONNIE: They could have called it 'Spatula' or 'Peanut Butter'. It doesn't matter what they call it.

ANNIE: [*something on her mind*] Bonnie …

BONNIE: Annie …

ANNIE: Bonnie …

BONNIE *looks at her, quizzically.* ANNIE *meets her gaze, but there's a slight sense of disquiet.*

Beat.

I think I saw Curtis.

BONNIE: You can't have.

ANNIE: I'm pretty sure it was Curtis.

BONNIE: Curtis hates dance.

ANNIE: He does, doesn't he?

BONNIE: Remember the fight we had after we made them go to the Pina Bausch documentary?

ANNIE: Curtis hated it!

BONNIE: And he told you at Pilates he wasn't going out. He was a long way from being able to socialise.

ANNIE: [*uneasily*] That's weird, 'cause he was standing at the bar with someone.

BONNIE: Who?

ANNIE: A woman.

BONNIE: What woman?

ANNIE: [*slightly sheepish*] A girl-woman.

BONNIE: What do you mean: 'girl-woman'?

CURTIS *swoops up to them.*

CURTIS: Bonnie! Annie!

BONNIE: Curtis!

CURTIS: Wow!

Kiss, kiss.

BONNIE and ANNIE: [*simultaneously*] Hey! / Hey.

CURTIS: Hey there.

Beat.

ANNIE: Hey.

CURTIS: Hey there.

ANNIE: Hey.

BONNIE: I didn't know you liked—?

CURTIS: No, I like it! I like it!

BONNIE: You don't like dance!

CURTIS: I like it! I'm loving it!

ANNIE: Amazing bodies.

CURTIS: Not like ballet dancers, are they? Some of the girls look like heifers. I mean that in a good way.

ANNIE: They're powerful bodies.

CURTIS: Powerful. Exactly. Love it. Love those powerful bodies.

Beat.

BONNIE [*unconvinced*] Fuck, Curtis. What the fuck?

She stares at him. He meets her gaze.

CURTIS: What, Bonnie? I'm allowed to— Okay … [*Defensive*] Someone asked me.

BONNIE: Yeah?

CURTIS: Yep.

Awkward beat.

BONNIE: [*a bit too aggressively*] Who?

Beat.

CURTIS: … Okay. Okay. Okay … A woman.

BONNIE: What woman?

CURTIS: A woman-woman. She's in the bathroom.

BONNIE: Do we know her, Curtis?

CURTIS: No, you don't, Bonnie … Well, Annie sort of does.

ANNIE *looks a bit compromised.*

Beat.

BONNIE: What's her name?

CURTIS: Greta.

ANNIE: [*a sense of inevitability*] Oh, wow.

BONNIE: 'Greta'?

CURTIS: Yes, Greta. Greta!

BONNIE: Isn't she—isn't she—?

Beat.

Oh, my God! … My God! Oh, my God!

CURTIS: Will you please stop saying that?!

ANNIE: The patisserie. The short film.

BONNIE: The ex-student?

CURTIS: It's really not a—

BONNIE: How ex, Curtis?

CURTIS: I taught her in Year Twelve.

BONNIE: When?

CURTIS: Ages ago!

BONNIE: What year?

CURTIS: Fuck, Bonnie! Jesus … [*Sheepishly*] Two years ago.

BONNIE: *Oh. My. God.* She's nineteen! She's nineteen? She's nineteen!

CURTIS: She's not nineteen! Fuck, Bonnie! She's not nineteen … she's twenty.

BONNIE: What deranged imbecile encouraged you to think hooking up with a twenty-year-old was an acceptable idea, Curtis?

CURTIS *realises with pleasure his upper hand.*

Beat.

CURTIS: Annie, actually.

ANNIE: Shit.

BONNIE: What?

CURTIS: Never did occur to me. I was frankly horrified. But Annie was very forceful.

ANNIE: Now, hang—

BONNIE: What!

ANNIE: [*to* BONNIE, *defensively*] It was actually your idea! You said I had to give him something to live for!

BONNIE: I meant a balloon ride! A wine course!

ANNIE: I thought you meant—

BONNIE: I can't believe you!

ANNIE: You said reconnect him with youth!

BONNIE: Jesus, Curtis—you should be on a fucking register!

CURTIS: Can we please not talk about this? Can we please not? Can we please withhold the judgement, thank you?

Long beat. Awkward. Everyone furious with everyone.

Sip of drinks. Finally:

BONNIE: Greta enjoying this?

CURTIS: [*defensively*] Yes, she is.

BONNIE: Did you get her one of those cushions to sit on so she could see?

CURTIS: No, she's quite tall, actually. And very mature.

BONNIE: Is that so?

CURTIS: She finds the 'democratic' concept of dance with the chunkier body type rather passé actually.

ANNIE: [*trying hard*] That's a point of view …

CURTIS: [*encouraged and infatuated*] She said: Once art was made by the best, the most beautiful? Why is elitism a dirty word?

ANNIE: Wow.

CURTIS: I thought that was rather interesting.

ANNIE: That *is* interesting.

BONNIE *shoots her a deadly look.*

BONNIE: I hear you moved out.

CURTIS: Serviced apartment.

BONNIE: How is it?

CURTIS: Noisy.

BONNIE: So things are actually going rather well for you then?

CURTIS: [*sharp, confident*] Yes, actually. There's actually something kind of transcendent about where I am right now. I was sitting there last night and I didn't have to explain myself. I didn't have to report: 'I'll clean up' or 'Think I might go up'. I can make a cup of tea without saying: 'Would you like one?' You have no idea what a liberation that is! I sat in front of the Netflix list and thought: life is actually one big Netflix list and from now on I can watch anything I like.

ANNIE: But Curtis … don't you miss her?

Beat. More vulnerability peeking through.

CURTIS: Yes, I miss her. I miss my beautiful Tess and her straight teeth and terrible spelling. I miss the way she folds cloth napkins and her tiny earlobes and her tap-dancing. But that Tess is gone.

CURTIS, *stressed, sees Greta in the distance and waves, indicating he's coming.* ANNIE *and* BONNIE *take her in.*

BONNIE: God, she is tall. Still growing, obviously.

The interval bell starts.

ANNIE and CURTIS: [*relieved*] There we go. / Drink after? / Oh, there's the bell!

SCENE SEVEN

TESS. *At home.*

TESS *attempts to put together an Ikea coffee table by trying to force two pieces of wood that don't fit and unable to make sense of the instructions.*

TESS: What the—? Fucking Swedish cocksucking rollmops.

She looks around to see if she's using one wrong bit but she's not.

Furious, she marches out of the room and comes back with an axe and starts chopping at the bits of timber: bam, bam, bam!

SCENE EIGHT

BONNIE *and* ANNIE. *At home. Later that night.*

BONNIE: Of course I'm telling Tess! Tess is my closest friend.

Beat.

ANNIE: Don't tell her, Bonnie! Take no position!

BONNIE: Isn't silence a position? What's so wonderful about withholding judgement? If we don't judge our friends, aren't we just setting them adrift in the world, rudderless?

ANNIE: That's ridiculous!

BONNIE: We're just greedy, mean, lustful, deceitful, naive members of the human race, constantly rationalising our own nasty appetites and we need people who tell us the truth.

ANNIE: Imagine if Tess told you the hard, cold truth about something. You think you'd be grateful?

BONNIE: It's hard to imagine her telling me something hurtful—

ANNIE: Exactly, because she's your friend!

BONNIE: Give me an example!

ANNIE: That's not the point!

BONNIE: What could Tess possibly say that was hurtful?

ANNIE: Anything!

BONNIE: What?!

ANNIE: Okay! Okay! What if she told you … that all your artists are lazy middle-class fakes?

BONNIE: [*shocked*] Why would she say that?

ANNIE: I'm saying, what if she said that?

BONNIE: She wouldn't, Annie! Because they're not! That's a stupid example. Tess respects what I do. [*Processing*] She's a big fan of my stable … a big fan.

She looks at ANNIE.

Do *you* think my artists are 'lazy middle-class fakes'?

ANNIE: [*the slightest shadow*] Of course I don't!

Beat. The seeds of doubt sewn.

I just thought the point of friends was kind of … to just reach out to them in times of need.

BONNIE: 'Reach out'?

ANNIE: Well …

BONNIE: What the fuck does that mean?

ANNIE: Alright!

BONNIE: Don't we have a duty to help them negotiate life? Don't we have a responsibility to steer them back when they blow off course? Any idiot can 'reach out'!

ANNIE: Okay, Bonnie!

BONNIE: So all Tess's crazy ideas I just accept?

ANNIE: I'm not saying that—

BONNIE: Yes, you are!

ANNIE: Well … they're not all crazy.

BONNIE: What does that mean?

ANNIE: I'm just saying that maybe, you know, they're not all crazy.

BONNIE: That's what you just said.

ANNIE: Okay, I just said it.

BONNIE: But what does it mean and don't say it a third time.

ANNIE: Don't do that!

BONNIE: Well?

ANNIE: [*a little uneasy*] I … kind of get it when Tess says … that questions need to be asked—

BONNIE Which questions?

ANNIE: [*defensively*] Just questions!

BONNIE: *What* questions, Annie?

ANNIE: The dynamic between people. Sometimes it's not healthy.

Beat.

BONNIE: Are you saying that our dynamic needs attention?

ANNIE: No. (Yes.)

BONNIE: Annie?

ANNIE: Sometimes, Bonnie, you don't take me seriously.

BONNIE: I take you very seriously when you avoid using clichés like 'reach out'.

ANNIE: There! There! There! That's what I'm talking about!

BONNIE: What?

ANNIE: That's the dynamic!

BONNIE: What dynamic?

ANNIE: The—the—the—the dynamic that could be something that two people look at …

BONNIE: Two people? What people?

ANNIE: Us people!

BONNIE: 'Us people'. Eloquence is your middle name!

ANNIE: There it is again!

BONNIE: There is what?

ANNIE: That! I can hear it! I can hear it! It's what you do—that thing—You know what I mean—

BONNIE: When you reach out to us people?

ANNIE: Fuck you! You think you can embarrass me into not growing?

They stare at each other in horror at where they have ended up.

Long beat.

BONNIE: What are we doing?

ANNIE: It's their fault!

BONNIE: Of course it's their fault, those fuckers!

ANNIE: We can't let them—

BONNIE: No way!

ANNIE: We have to 'detach'.

BONNIE: Absolutely.

ANNIE: If we're ever caught up with them and things get ugly—

BONNIE: We just get the hell out!

ANNIE: [*thinking*] Listen, we'll have a code word … Say, if I say … 'Flat battery', then we know we have to get out of there.

BONNIE: 'Flat battery'?

ANNIE: Flat battery.

Beat. They look at each other tenderly. They kiss.

BONNIE: Annie—

ANNIE: Bonnie—

BONNIE: I love you. I don't say that often enough.

SCENE NINE

TESS *and* CURTIS.

TESS: [*a little shy*] Kiss me.

CURTIS: Tess—

TESS: Just because we're splitting, doesn't mean affectionate gestures should go. Don't you think?

CURTIS: It's—I don't know—I'm ambivalent.

TESS: Ambivalent?

CURTIS: It's a bit of a mixed message.

TESS: You won't kiss me?

CURTIS: Not right now. I'm not a yoyo.

TESS: Okay.

Beat.

I was asked on a date.

A bit of an eyebrow lift from CURTIS.

He wanted to do tapas.

CURTIS: Is that a euphemism?

She misreads his expression as stoicism.

TESS: I just think full disclosure is the only way. I know it's painful. But—for all our faults, we've always been honest with each other.

CURTIS: [*hurt*] Full disclosure.

TESS: An acquaintance set us up.

CURTIS: What 'acquaintance'?

TESS: It doesn't matter. She wouldn't take no for an answer. Saddle up, she said.

CURTIS: Saddle up?

TESS: Obviously I'm not remotely interested. I told her. I said: I'm not ready to saddle up.

CURTIS: That's Bonnie's phrase. Bonnie says 'saddle up'!

TESS: It wasn't Bonnie, alright it *was* Bonnie. I told her I had no interest but you know what she's like.

CURTIS: A stablehand?

TESS: He's in I.T.. Boring! Of course I said no. That's not what this is about.

CURTIS: I can't believe it was Bonnie!

TESS: Leave Bonnie out of this. The point is he'd never heard of Tony Blair!

CURTIS: He asked you out and you talked about Tony Blair?

TESS: I don't know. It just came up. And he said: He's that TV chef, right? [*A game show 'wrong answer' noise:*] *Baaaahhhhh!*

CURTIS *isn't laughing but it's not for the reason* TESS *thinks. She's very empathetic to how he might feel about this.*

I miss you.

CURTIS: That's good.

TESS: Babe …

She looks at him with love and pity and tenderness. Struggling to find the words.

[*Tenderly*] I know this is hard. But you'll get used to it.
CURTIS: Alright.
TESS: And you know … I really believe this will be good for us.
CURTIS: Okay.
TESS: No-one's saying … Well, you know.
CURTIS: No.
TESS: This is what I need to do right now.
CURTIS: I get that.
TESS: But no-one's saying … it has to be forever.

CURTIS *looks at her uncomprehendingly: What the fuck?*

CURTIS: [*in cold fury*] You wreak havoc. And then you say—you say—maybe the havoc is just temporary?
TESS: No! No! Look—no. No. I get that you're angry, Curtis.

From left: Peter Houghton as Curtis and Catherine McClements as Tess in the Melbourne Theatre Company 2017 production. (Photo: Jeff Busby)

CURTIS: How big a grave do I dig, Tess? To bury our union? Because if I'm going to have to dig it out again, will a shallow grave do?

TESS: I'm just saying … you know, the Amish kids—

CURTIS: What Amish kids?

TESS: *'Rumspringa'*. The Amish practice of allowing the kids, when they hit adolescence, to run amok. Technology and sex and drugs and driving Ford Fiestas instead of buggies.

CURTIS: What does this have to do with anything?

TESS: They have the choice after that year, to leave the church or to come back and sign up. And ninety per cent of them choose to come back. When we turn forty, we should all have a *rumspringa*. Us couples. Permission to go crazy. And maybe what we would find is that we actually like imprisonm—*belonging*.

CURTIS: You want to drive a Ford Fiesta, Tess?

TESS: [*ignoring him*] Wouldn't it make sense, Curtis? For forty-something accountants or—or midwives—just normal people to have *rumspringa*? [*Tenderly*] Look, you have to 'catch up' with me. It's unfair. But in couples, one is always one step ahead and then the other has to get up to speed.

CURTIS: So we're still a couple?

TESS: No, we're not a couple.

CURTIS: We're not a couple but this is how it is with couples?

TESS: I'm not going to argue with you about terminology! I'm saying that when I do start seeing other people, in the future, it will be hard but you'll manage. You will get up to speed, Curtis. I promise you.

He looks at her. She takes in the pause, the gaze.

CURTIS: I'm seeing someone.

TESS: I think that's a great idea. You've never been good at talking about your feelings.

CURTIS *makes the same noise* TESS *made with relation to a wrong answer.*

CURTIS: [*wrong answer buzzer*] *Baaaahhhhh!*

TESS *looks at him, confused.*

I have a new sexual partner I'm having sex with. It's sexual.

Beat.

TESS: What?

Beat.

Is this a joke?

CURTIS *is silent.* TESS *starts laughing.*

CURTIS: She's twenty. I taught her. She's very thin. But with big, highly sprung breasts.

TESS: That is a joke. Isn't it?

CURTIS: [*arch*] I get that you feel as if you have to 'catch up' with me. It's unfair. But you will get up to speed, Tess. I promise you.

She stares at him in disbelief.

Greta. The filmmaker who hates everything.

TESS: [*shocked and in horror*] I don't believe it. I don't believe it. I don't. I don't. I just don't believe it. It's unbelievable … You're seeing … you're seeing a twenty-year-old? Why don't you just take Lola out? It makes economic sense, Curtis. Combine dating with child support!

CURTIS: That's disgusting!

TESS: You're disgusting! She's not much more than a teenager!

CURTIS: I know. *It's fantastic.* Do you know what I wonder, Tess? I get it that people come together to make more people—it's fundamental to the survival of the species. But enduring love—that's not fundamental. That's just a conceit dreamt up by poets. It's just … irrational optimism.

TESS: Irrational optimism can work!

CURTIS: Can it?

TESS: Once upon a time, you hocked your vinyl to buy me a ring! Now you're dating a—

CURTIS: You threw us away! You— [*Astonished, his eye caught by* TESS*'s wrist*] What is that?

Beat.

You got a tattoo? … You hate tattoos …

TESS: It was spontaneous.

CURTIS: What is it?

TESS: The candlestick.

CURTIS: Tess—

TESS: Can't you see I'm struggling? If you cared about me you'd be patient! You'd wait for me! You wouldn't just fall into bed with the first bimbo that crossed your path!

CURTIS: She's no bimbo. She's fully cognisant of Tony Blair for starters.

TESS, *about to continue her diatribe, suddenly stops.*

TESS: My God …

Beat. Thinking ... more thinking ...

[*A moment of realisation*] You wanted this!

CURTIS What?!

TESS: You wanted this! In your heart of hearts, you wanted this, Curtis. [*With new insight*] That's what you do! You decide what you want and then you steer me into initiating it so that you're not the bad guy.

CURTIS: I'm *not* the bad guy!

TESS: You manipulate me into actions you secretly covet!

CURTIS: I didn't covet breaking up, Tess. You coveted it and you got it, because you always get what you want!

TESS: Before my yearnings—let's not call them that anymore—you started emotionally withdrawing— You knew I wanted more.

CURTIS: You always want more.

TESS: I wanted to be alive to you. I wanted to be a presence. I didn't want to be an inevitability. I wanted sex to be better because of our emotional intimacy, not worse for it.

CURTIS: It was better!

TESS: Bullshit! Sex is always better with someone who's a mystery.

CURTIS: How do you know that?

TESS: Well, *isn't it?*

Beat. Their eyes meet.

The imagination is legal infidelity. Not doing it is just short-changing yourself, it's like paying for a buffet and eating a canapé. And I know you get that. Because the moment I became a mother, on some level I became *your* mother.

CURTIS: That's garbage! That's psycho-crap!

TESS: Every time you called me Mum with Lola … 'Mummy's getting dressed' or 'Mum will pick you up', it was a dagger in our sex life!

CURTIS: But everyone does that!

TESS: The lover can't be the mother! The mother is everything the lover isn't. The better I got at being a mother, the further our erotic lives disappeared.

CURTIS: Let's get one thing straight—when we fucked I did not feel as if you were my mother!

TESS: But I did.

Long sad beat.

CURTIS: I loved sex with you. I'm not going to sully that. And waking up next to you did it for me. Every fucking morning I was delighted you were there. I didn't need to say it. I didn't need to hold a symposium. I didn't need to change a thing. I always desired you. But now I couldn't get an erection if I tried, because the woman I loved has become subsumed in accumulated disappointment. In herself and in me.

TESS: [*deeply hurt and shocked*] That's … cruel.

Beat.

She looks at him: Is this true?

A catastrophic new low. It's so much worse than anything she ever expected.

[*Quietly, heartbroken*] I didn't want to destroy anything. I wanted us to go out there and discover something.

CURTIS: [*refusing to soften*] Well, I've gone out there and I've discovered something *better than you*.

TESS *bursts into tears.*

TESS: I loved you. Curtis. Curtis. I loved you. I loved you. I loved you. You loved me. We loved each other. Why are you—why is this … How can we …? How can we …?

Beat.

CURTIS *is moved by this but determined not to buckle. He passes her the box of tissues. She blows her nose. She absorbs his refusal to weaken.*

She is utterly devastated but with a huge struggle, she attempts to pull herself together.

How did you first—how did you first contact her?

CURTIS: Tess—

TESS: I want to know! I have a right to know!

CURTIS: She called me.

TESS: She called you?

CURTIS: Annie gave her my number.

Beat.

TESS: Annie?

CURTIS: Annie.

TESS: *Annie gave Greta your number?*

CURTIS: Yes.

TESS: How did—how did Annie have Greta's number?

CURTIS: Remember the patisserie? When she invited you both to her short film?

Beat as TESS *takes this in.*

TESS: [*through gritted teeth*] Where were you?

CURTIS: At school. I was in the chapel. My phone rang. It was Greta. Is that enough of a picture?

TESS: [*shocked*] In the chapel? How tasteful! Where people get married!

CURTIS: What are you talking about? *We* didn't get married in a church. Your conversational party piece is: Religion is the biggest terrorist of all.

TESS: What do you mean: 'party piece'?

CURTIS: Just that! Just that! You have a number of lines you pull out when you want to establish your intellectual prowess.

TESS: I don't need 'lines', Curtis. I have intellectual prowess!

CURTIS: Spell 'prowess'.

TESS: Fuck you!

CURTIS: How many times have you said it, Tess? 'Religion is the biggest terrorist of all'. How all football matches are 'fixed'. That's another one.

TESS: They are fixed, Curtis!

CURTIS: I've fucking heard it, Tess!

TESS: I can't believe she—

CURTIS: What?

TESS: Wants you.

CURTIS: Now, you're just being nasty!

TESS: She's cool.

CURTIS: I'm cool!

TESS: You deliberately wear mismatched socks.

CURTIS: That's witty and—and—irreverent.

TESS: You never miss 'Call the Midwife'. Does she know that? … And you don't make money.

CURTIS: I make money.

TESS: You're a teacher.

CURTIS: Okay. Okay. Now, we're getting somewhere!

TESS: It never mattered to me, Curtis—but I don't think a teacher's salary is a major drawcard to sexy girls who 'want things'.

CURTIS: It obviously did matter to you!

TESS: Greta and her pals—they love money! They're all about money! They can talk about art all they like but it's money they value. And status. Young people are very into qualifications. They all have three or four degrees to qualify for long-term unemployment! And exactly the moment you get the PhD she forces you into, she's going to go off with the lead singer of a very hip band. Because one day he might be worth millions, but you're definitely never going to be worth more than a one-bedroom flat.

CURTIS: [*unsure*] Greta and I can be happy in a one-bedroom flat.

TESS: That's what *we* said. Twenty years ago. So we both know it's not true … Imagine the boredom of having to explain things to her … Her friends whose youth seems so cheerful and uplifting until it's just really annoying … And after a while the reality is going to hit you that if you date someone the same age as your daughter, no-one you like likes you.

CURTIS: [*incensed*] You said: We're over. You loved me, yada, yada, but you needed more, you needed something, you couldn't articulate but it had wonder in it and searching and growing. There was no 'going back'. I thought to myself, well I actually think wonder and searching and growing is … horseshit. So it was going to be hard to jump on that particular bandwagon with you. But I agree the tick is getting louder. To me that means spend less time arguing and more time doing. And lo and behold along comes this lovely young woman, not a million miles away from you before you got mean, and she says: You're interesting. We could have some old-fashioned fun together. And let me give you the best blow job you've ever had. (No false promise there, by the way.) Have I painted that picture well enough? Now stop for a moment and ask yourself: Who started this story?

TESS: If you'd seen me. If you'd seen me. If you opened your eyes and saw me—

CURTIS: I did see you, Tess. I saw your hypocrisy and your competitiveness and how easily threatened you are. I saw your ability to vent your professional frustrations on Lola because you can really do a shitload of damage if you want to and there have been times you wanted to. For a lovely, beautiful woman you were actually pretty fucking ghastly in a lot of ways. But I was there. I was by your side.

This is like a physical blow to TESS. *She seems to physically crumble.*

TESS: I'm not lovable.

CURTIS: What?

TESS: That's why you're doing this. Because I'm not lovable. I'm not lovable. I'm not lovable.

CURTIS: You don't trust I love you. So you inflict the biggest possible damage and if I'm still there, then you've discovered something. And I failed the test because it's your shit, not mine. And the big irony here—the really funny if it wasn't tragic irony here—is that I did love you. I did love you. But I don't love you anymore.

She falls to the floor, utterly and completely bereft.

He watches her silently. He's spent. He's exhausted. He can't bear it. She's lost. She sees no hope, no redemption.

He walks towards her as if he might just, possibly, comfort her. She is suspended inside a glimmer of hope when:

I'm taking the tantalus.

Beat. She looks up at him.

TESS [*incredulous*] What?

CURTIS: Just that and my own personal books and records.

TESS: You're kidding.

CURTIS: No.

TESS: The tantalus?

CURTIS: Yes.

She starts laughing at the absurdity.

TESS: Grandpa Harper's tantalus?

CURTIS: Yes.

TESS: *My* grandpa's tantalus?

CURTIS: Your mother left it to me. It's mine. Legally.

TESS: You're not taking the tantalus, Curtis.

CURTIS: I'm afraid I am, Tess.

TESS: My mother left it to you because you were her son-in-law.

CURTIS: No. She left it to me because she liked me.

TESS: [*trying to stay calm*] Curtis. Curtis. Curtis. That's my family—it doesn't mean anything to you.

CURTIS: How do you know?

TESS: It's been in my family since the 1860s. It's a sentimental family heirloom and you're not having it. I'll buy you a tantalus. I'll buy you any tantalus you like.

CURTIS: I don't want an eBay tantalus!

TESS: I was thinking of a fancy antique emporium, you bastard.

CURTIS: Bullshit, you were thinking of some eBay tantalus with missing bits from some sheep farmer in Norfolk.

TESS: I don't care how much it costs. But you're not having this one.

CURTIS: It's just a thing.

TESS: So why do you want it?

CURTIS: I don't have to justify why I want to keep something that's mine.

TESS: You can't have the tantalus.

CURTIS: I think I'm in love.

A sudden stop to proceedings.

Despite her rage, this is utterly devastating to TESS.

I can't explain it … but I will. It's a feeling of intense … invigoration. I realise now that I always felt as if you made me successful. The fact you chose me bestowed success on me. Then you left and I realised that I'm actually a reasonably successful person without you. I feel as if I've been living in, say, Ottawa all my life and I've suddenly parachuted into … Barcelona. There's this thrilling kind of buzz in my bloodstream that's like a really good, expensive alcohol, and when I wake up next to Greta, I feel as if I'm inside a really classy ad written by a European copywriter.

Her devastation and shock gives him another boost for his finale:

I suddenly got it. What you've been trying to make me understand. I looked into her face and I got it. With you I'm destined to the same fate as *Madame Bovary:* The future was a dark corridor, and at the far end the door was bolted.

Beat.

Tess, she unbolts that door.

SCENE TEN

Annie and Bonnie's place.

TESS, ANNIE, BONNIE. ANNIE *being grilled by a slightly unhinged* TESS.

TESS: Half a fucking brain? A quarter?

ANNIE: [*very uncomfortable*] Tess …

TESS: Or are there just rocks up there?

ANNIE: Look, I'm sorry.

TESS: Is your brain completely empty or are you actually malevolent? Do you hate me, Annie?

ANNIE: Tess! God! Okay!

BONNIE: She misunderstood.

TESS: Oh, okay! Okay then! Okay! You suggested she find Curtis a middle-aged fuck-buddy and she misunderstood and got him a twenty-year-old?

ANNIE and BONNIE: [*simultaneously*] No! / Shit! / God! / That's not it!

BONNIE: I wanted Annie to remind him that life goes on.

TESS: Well, thanks so much for the vast support of The Sisterhood. You're worrying about Curtis's love life while I'm getting missives from his lawyer, Bertie Fucking Wooster!

BONNIE: Tessie …

TESS: It's been one month! After twenty years! His side of the bed still smells of him.

ANNIE: God. Tess—

TESS: [*distressed*] He wouldn't get a lawyer unless—

ANNIE: It's her—She's probably—

BONNIE: It's him—'Mr Nice Guy!' Happens every time!

TESS: [*distraught and vulnerable*] Twenty years! And he's already moved on!

BONNIE: Honey—You wanted this.

TESS: I didn't want this! I didn't want this!

BONNIE: You're better off without him!

TESS: I didn't want this!

BONNIE: [*a little tough*] Then what did you want?

TESS *looks at* BONNIE*, bereft.*

TESS: Just … *more* …

BONNIE: You want to find something out, don't you? Who you are in the deepest way? Who Curtis is?

TESS: I do … I do! I do!

BONNIE: This is a very immature reaction to him taking the reins. But it doesn't fundamentally alter what you want. Which is to … find something out.

TESS: You're right … You're right … I do want to find something out … But what if I find out … what if … [*With horror*] What if there's nothing to find out? … What if we're our best selves … with each other?

ANNIE *and* BONNIE *catch each other's eye—an awkward moment.*

I have to have someone with me when we're dividing things. Will you be there, Bonnie?

BONNIE: Of course I'll be there!

TESS: [*forgiving her*] And you'll be there for me too, Annie?

Awkward. Not the moment to tell her that Curtis has already asked.

ANNIE: Mmmm … I'll be there.

TESS: [*suddenly very, very tough*] He wants the tantalus.

BONNIE: No way!

ANNIE: What's a 'tantalus'?

BONNIE: The decanter thing. The thingo with the Scotch thing.

ANNIE: Oh! Wasn't that your grandfather's?

TESS: Yes, it was!

BONNIE: [*to* ANNIE] Her mother left it to Curtis.

ANNIE: Why would she do that?

TESS: Because she was unhinged!

BONNIE: This is crazy. You're talking about *things*, already?

TESS: Everyone talks about things! Everyone keeps saying to me: What about the house?

ANNIE: What is happening to the house?

TESS: See! See!

ANNIE: No, but—

BONNIE: He's not getting the house!

TESS: He'll get the house! He'll get the house! He'll take the tantalus! He'll take all of it! He's getting removalists! He's making lists!

BONNIE: He's not getting the house!

TESS: He said he's entitled.

ANNIE: Well, it probably is true that—

TESS: [*not expecting this*] What?

ANNIE: He probably is … entitled.

BONNIE: Annie!

TESS: Mum and Dad paid the deposit!

ANNIE: [*sheepishly*] I'm not saying … It's just the law.

BONNIE: The law?

ANNIE: Everyone knows things are divided fifty-fifty.

BONNIE: [*irritated*] Not when it's the woman who paid for everything!

ANNIE: Yes, even when it's the woman.

BONNIE: That can't be right!

ANNIE: [*steadfastly*] Curtis is entitled to half the house.

TESS: [*a scream of despair*] Aaaarghhhhhh!

BONNIE: But she bought the house! It was her money!

ANNIE: Well, we fought for equality back when men were the earners.

BONNIE: That's not the kind of equality we wanted!

ANNIE: Well, this is what we won. Equal status.

BONNIE: Even when the men earn less?

TESS: It's okay, Bonnie!

BONNIE: That's absurd!

ANNIE: It's the law, Bonnie!

TESS: Look, can you—?

BONNIE: How do you know so much about this anyway?

ANNIE: What are you saying?

BONNIE: I'm wondering how—?

ANNIE: I'm allowed to be informed!

BONNIE: This is a bit too informed for you!

TESS: Listen, you two—

ANNIE: 'For you'?

BONNIE: Yes, for you! Yes, for you!

ANNIE: They both contributed!

BONNIE: But she contributed more!

ANNIE: Bonnie—

BONNIE: Annie—

TESS: Annie—Bonnie—

ANNIE: There are lots of ways of measuring 'contribution'. It's not just about who pays the bills, Bonnie!

BONNIE: So the fact that she worked hard and aspired and had ambitions and reaped the rewards has no ultimate bearing on what she is due?

ANNIE: What are you saying?

BONNIE: What are *you* saying?

ANNIE: What are *you* saying?

TESS: Listen—this is actually—

ANNIE: Do you think I contribute less to our life together because I make thirty dollars an hour?

BONNIE: Yes. Financially.

ANNIE: Fuck you!

BONNIE: That's just a fact. It's not a put-down. It's *actual*.

ANNIE: I tell you what else is actual! I make our house a home.

BONNIE: Of course you do! I know that! But we wouldn't have a home if we didn't have a house and we wouldn't have a house if I didn't have a big fat fucking salary.

TESS: Would it be okay if we got back to me? Is that okay? Is it alright with you two? If we just come back to me for a moment because my life has completely fallen apart? …

Beat as BONNIE *and* ANNIE, *both simmering with fury, turn back to* TESS.

I said: What entitles you? What makes you think that a cheating fucker is entitled to anything?

ANNIE: He's not exactly cheating …

TESS: [*furiously*] Why do you keep apologising for him?

BONNIE: Exactly! God, Annie!

ANNIE: I'm just saying that you left, Tess, so … I guess … he's not cheating.

BONNIE: You're *endorsing*—?

ANNIE: I'm not endorsing, I'm pointing out—

TESS: Annie, what is your problem?

ANNIE: You can always buy him out of the tantalus, Tess.

BONNIE: Why should she buy him out?!

ANNIE: Because it's his tantalus!

BONNIE: It was her grandfather's!

TESS: He doesn't love the tantalus. *I* love the tantalus.

BONNIE: Of course he doesn't!

ANNIE: I'm just saying that technically—

BONNIE: 'Technically'!

ANNIE: Yes, technically it's—

TESS: It's my tantalus! It's my tantalus! It was my grandfather's! It's a family heirloom! Bonnie, get Curtis to give me the tantalus!

BONNIE: You bet I will!

TESS: Tell him to have some decency!

BONNIE: Absolutely, I will!

TESS: Do what you have to, Bonnie, but I want the tantalus!

SCENE ELEVEN

CURTIS *and* BONNIE. *Each cradling a drink.*

CURTIS: Bonnie … Look. Maybe I did contribute … Maybe I—I don't know—didn't pay attention. There were times I probably did … close down, or something.

BONNIE: That's honest.

CURTIS: I probably felt more secure than I should have and that made me … complacent … She's probably right about that. And I don't really know what I'm doing with … It's just … Trying to boost myself or something horribly shallow … Some desperate bid to feel alive again … And maybe without even realising it I want to hurt her …

BONNIE: Curtis. God. You know, we want you to know that you're equally important to us.

CURTIS: Thanks, Bon.

BONNIE: The fact is, you're both our friends. We want you to be okay. We haven't stopped loving you. That would be impossible. There's too much history.

CURTIS: I appreciate that you care. I really do. And I'm actually really happy that you care for her. I mean, she can be very, very tough but we're all human. Some more than others. Her, perhaps a bit less. But she needs friends …

BONNIE: [*slightly jokey*] And you don't?

CURTIS: No, of course. Of course I do. Yes. And I hope we are friends.

BONNIE: Of course we're friends. That's what I'm saying.

CURTIS: I certainly don't need any more mothers!

BONNIE: [*vaguely affronted*] I don't think we're mothering you!

CURTIS: No?

BONNIE: We're simply pointing out that provocation is not helping.

Beat.

CURTIS: Provocation?

BONNIE: The lawyer.

Beat. Distinct tension suddenly in the air.

CURTIS: [*calmly*] Well, well, well— Ah, she left me, Bonnie. Wouldn't you say that was the provocation?!

BONNIE: I think you could afford to be a little bit more generous in relation to certain objects.

CURTIS: Objects?

He studies BONNIE.

Long beat as they hold each other's gaze.

[*Cottoning on*] I know what this is about. She sent you.

BONNIE: What?

CURTIS: She sent you! *Tess sent you!*

BONNIE: She never sent me.

CURTIS: She sent you! She sent you!

BONNIE: She did not send me.

CURTIS She sent you, Bonnie!

BONNIE: Okay, she sent me! Big deal, Curtis!

CURTIS: Bonnie … Bonnie, Bonnie, Bonnie … Why are you doing her bidding?

BONNIE: Why didn't you tell her about Greta until after we busted you?

CURTIS: You didn't 'bust me' and for the same reasons nobody does! Because I didn't want trouble. Because I didn't want to hurt her. Because I wasn't sure what I was doing. And then—then—then I didn't tell her because—because— Fuck it! Because, Bonnie—I'm mad with her!

BONNIE: You should have confessed about Greta and Tess would have taken you back and you, relieved, forgiven, would have continued on, invigorated by your bad behaviour, but also wizened to what mattered. And then we wouldn't be in this mess.

CURTIS: 'We'.

BONNIE: We're in it, too! We're in this shit knee-deep, you fucker! And you know it! God, Curtis, you made Lola. You had a daughter, Curtis!

CURTIS: I realise that, Bonnie! We're not the first!

BONNIE: And we're her godparents, by the way. We are invested in her wellbeing. We are inextricably linked.

CURTIS: Yes, we are.

BONNIE: Do you remember when we first met at Annie's dad's funeral? And she was so terrified we wouldn't like each other? And you said to me in the carpark: I'm reserving judgement, but if you hurt her, I will hunt you down and kill you slowly.

CURTIS: And you smiled.

BONNIE: Because I knew that you and I were the only two people on the planet who loved her that much.

Beat as they absorb that.

And the four of us went to The Punters' Club and Tess and I got talking and it was like meeting my soul mate. And the love you demonstrated for each other and the respect you showed, the way you laughed so authentically at each other's jokes and spurred each other on to tell stories or—or—express opinions. You were *proud* of each other. *I was in love with your love affair*. You two showed me how good it could be, how much better it was to have someone next to you. Do you realise that?

CURTIS: [*affected by this*] Alright, Bonnie …

BONNIE: [*with passionate conviction*] My God, Curtis! You climbed Everest together. You got over the chaos of falling in love and resentment and need and foibles and never enough money and children and work issues and money issues and when it seemed impossible to climb that mountain you two somehow did it. Together. And then three metres from the summit you say: Fuck it. I'm going down.

CURTIS: It's not three metres, Bonnie. We're in our forties.

BONNIE: Okay then. You're halfway up.

CURTIS: *She* was the one who decided to forgo the summit as you well know.

BONNIE If you'd supported her … if you'd lent her your oxygen mask …

CURTIS: Thanks for the pep talk but I was all out of oxygen too, as it happens. And now I want to climb the next half with Greta … And I've bought myself a Kathmandu backpack and inside it is the tantalus.

SCENE TWELVE

Annie and Bonnie's. ANNIE *and* BONNIE, CURTIS *and* TESS. *Fast.*

BONNIE: Yoga program 'Greet the Dawn'—not refundable. Or the Bhut'n-gluten-free cooking class. I checked with her supervisor.

TESS: So what you're saying is—

BONNIE: Part-refund on accommodation, but not flights as it was a group booking—

CURTIS: It's ages away!

ANNIE: Not really—

CURTIS: That's ridiculous—

BONNIE: You can try, be my guest—

CURTIS: I've never heard of such a thing— Can I have a drink?

BONNIE: They had to sell a certain number of seats and it was on that basis—No you can't.

ANNIE: Fine print, obviously—

CURTIS: No-one reads that—

BONNIE: But we signed the 'Accept Conditions' box—

CURTIS: This is bullshit! Who are these people?

ANNIE: Bhutan specialists.

CURTIS: What a scam.

BONNIE: Actually pretty common with these things—

CURTIS: So that's sixteen hundred down the gurgler?

BONNIE: Plus half the accom on the hotel, which was half board by the way, and the river cruise is no refund, and then the Airbnb was one of the strict cancellations, so we do get something back on that but once it goes three ways—that's weird saying that—three ways—then it's probably less than a couple of hundred dollars.

CURTIS: We were Airbnb'ing in Bhutan?

BONNIE: Yes, we were.

CURTIS: What, there are Airbnb caves? I thought the point was to do it cheaply?

BONNIE: It would have been cheaply if we did it. It's not cheap because we're not doing it. What happened was you two decided to just fuck everything up.

TESS: I don't think that's—

CURTIS: I need the money, Bonnie!

BONNIE: 'And thank you, Bonnie, for your efforts to secure us all visas which was extremely time-consuming and in the end, pointless.'

ANNIE: Did you have insurance?

CURTIS: What insurance?

ANNIE: Travel insurance?

CURTIS: I was going to remind Tess about travel insurance but I got distracted by the savage mockery she made of her marriage vows.

BONNIE: Grow up, my friend.

CURTIS: I didn't anticipate cancelling.

ANNIE: Curtis, that's *why* you get travel insurance.

CURTIS: You have insurance—?

ANNIE: Sure, we have insurance.

BONNIE: Obviously we have insurance.

CURTIS: You got it for yourselves?

ANNIE: Curtis. We love you but we don't include you on our insurance cover, no.

CURTIS *looks at* TESS.

CURTIS: Do you have insurance?

TESS: No.

CURTIS: You always handled the insurance. You realise we are each sixteen hundred down, Tess?

TESS: Yes, I do.

CURTIS: Doesn't that bother you?

TESS: Not really … [*A new thought*] I don't like 'always'.

CURTIS: 'Always' is *why* people get married. With 'always', the travel insurance gets done.

ANNIE: I don't think blame is useful.

CURTIS: I'm finding it useful.

BONNIE: You know what, Curtis, you are sounding more and more like a jerk.

CURTIS: You're the one railroaded us into Bhutan. Who wants Bhutan? Bonnie wants Bhutan! Curtis would actually like New York or even Paris. Predictable I know, but not the epicentre of global dysentery. But no, no, no, Bhutan Beckons Bonnie!

TESS: [*on autopilot*] Off we go to Bhutan!

BONNIE: Someone has to make a decision. You're all scared of making decisions.

ANNIE: Maybe we'd actually like the opportunity to make a decision. If we're given the chance.

BONNIE: *Once*, you made a decision! One time you took charge because I was running the art fair. And look how that worked out!

CURTIS: Not this again!

TESS: That was really awful.

ANNIE: I got confused!

BONNIE: North and South Korea? We get on the train in Beijing, and lo and behold it's all aboard for Pyongyang!

CURTIS: The point is Tess should be taking the rap for this costly debacle!

TESS: The moment I got the e-ticket to Bhutan was when I realised Curtis and I had to end.

BONNIE: What?

TESS: I didn't want to go to Bhutan but here I was with an e-ticket in my inbox. I didn't want to be standing in kitchens chopping carrots, but there I am, night after night. I don't want to find Curtis irritating or predictable or petty and yet I do feel that. I had to ask myself: Why am I always ending up in situations I don't really want?

CURTIS: You could have just said: I don't want to go to Bhutan.

SCENE THIRTEEN

Bonnie and Annie's place. BONNIE *and* ANNIE.

BONNIE: Really?

ANNIE: 'Really'? Why are you saying it like that? 'Really'?

BONNIE: No! Great! Where did this come from?

ANNIE: Well … [*Proud of this*] We're too dependent on other people. It's not good. It's not healthy. It's unreliable. We have to be able to survive alone.

BONNIE: … Alone?

ANNIE: Alone, together.

BONNIE: … Okay. Sure. I've always told you professional development is important.

ANNIE: No, this is nothing to do with health sciences.

BONNIE [*an old point reiterated*] Annie. Massage is not a 'health science'.

ANNIE: In your opinion!

BONNIE: No, actually, not in—

ANNIE: [*interrupting*] Law.

Beat.

BONNIE *is unable to stem the incredulity.*

BONNIE: You're starting law?

ANNIE: You're doing that again! [*Imitating her intonation*] 'Law?' 'Law?' 'Law?'

BONNIE: Okay!

ANNIE: I'm going to be a lawyer.

BONNIE: Wow.

ANNIE: Yes.

BONNIE: Law?

ANNIE: Yes.

BONNIE: That's quite an undertaking, Annie.

ANNIE: I realise that, Bonnie. I realise it's an undertaking and I'm undertaking it.

Beat.

[*Noting* BONNIE*'s silence*] What?

BONNIE: No—that's wonderful— Where are you doing this?

ANNIE: Online.

BONNIE: You can do law online?

ANNIE: Yes.

BONNIE: That's … accessible.

ANNIE: Fuck, Bonnie! God!

BONNIE: Okay! Okay! Great! Great! Be a lawyer!
ANNIE: 'Be a lawyer'?
BONNIE: Be a lawyer! Be a lawyer!
ANNIE: The way you say that! Like I'm doing it to annoy you!
BONNIE: I'm giving you my blessing!
ANNIE: So that's the green light then? Your blessing?
BONNIE: [*frustrated*] I'm saying: Be a lawyer!
ANNIE: You know, you know, you know, any time I get excited about anything you—you—you say something to burst my balloon. Always. When I wanted to do carpentry. Or French horn. Or get a baby kitten!
BONNIE: It's just a kitten. Not a baby kitten.
ANNIE: You want me to stay the same. I don't know why!
BONNIE: Most people complain the other person wants to change them!
ANNIE: You don't want me to evolve from who I was!
BONNIE: 'From who I was' is implied in 'evolve'.
ANNIE: Fuck you!
BONNIE: Annie, I fell in love with you! I don't want you to start yearning and become something different!
ANNIE: Something better!
BONNIE: Maybe not! Maybe you'll go from being an excellent and contented masseuse to a lousy and miserable lawyer!
ANNIE: That's inspiring!
BONNIE: Humans are hardly ever good at what they want to be. I wanted to be an artist and I was terrible!
ANNIE: [*matter of fact*] That's because you don't have any imagination. If you had imagination, you'd be great.
BONNIE: I don't have any imagination?

Beat as BONNIE *absorbs this, more confused than mad.*

ANNIE: I'm saying you could do anything you wanted to do, Bonnie, if you had the talent.
BONNIE: Annie … don't you realise? … we're living in a house of cards and if one person pulls a card out of the middle, the whole thing comes down. Everyone would be happier if we grew into someone and stayed that person.
ANNIE: This is about fear!

BONNIE: Okay okay okay okay—it's about fear.
ANNIE: I make you feel smart and successful.

Beat.

BONNIE: [*surprised*] Isn't that good?
ANNIE: Not if it makes me feel dumb and a failure.

BONNIE *walks up to* ANNIE, *gently takes her hand and looks sincerely into her eyes.*

Beat.

BONNIE: I think it would be fantastic if you did a law degree.
ANNIE: You have no faith in me.

BONNIE *lets go of her hand, frustrated.*

BONNIE: Maybe I have no faith in you. Maybe I think, on the law of averages, that it's highly unlikely a masseuse will become a great lawyer and I'm going to have to watch a lot of television on my own while you are studying for exams you end up failing and then comforting you while paying for your pointless higher education.

Beat.

Or maybe I have so much faith in you that I can imagine you getting your degree and landing a job at the U.N. and giving Ted talks and falling in love with someone young and cute and blonde like Greta and you will be young and cute together while I get old and fat.
ANNIE: Well… which one is it?

They stare at each other: ANNIE *trying to read* BONNIE, BONNIE *trying to understand herself.* BONNIE*'s confidence is momentarily shaken.*

BONNIE: [*vulnerable, simply*] I know I'm hard to love. Someone—out there—might love you better, Annie, but no-one will love you more.

ANNIE *moves towards her.*

Together, they come to a tender kiss.

They stop and look at each other.

[*Plaintively*] Can't we go back, Annie? Can't we go back to before? Can't we glue Tess and Curtis back together? Can't we go to Bhutan?

SCENE FOURTEEN

Tess and Curtis's house. TESS *and* CURTIS.

Energy is high. We are mid-conversation:

CURTIS: Buy me out.

TESS: Buy you out?

CURTIS: Buy me out.

TESS: You're kidding me?

CURTIS: Not kidding. Buy me out.

TESS: On an editor's salary?

CURTIS: What about the money from your mother?

TESS: That's in trust for Lola. I can't touch it! And I don't want to touch it!

CURTIS: Then we sell the house.

TESS: What?

CURTIS: We can both get something smaller.

TESS: [*panicked*] We won't both get anything smaller, Curtis. We won't get anything at all!

CURTIS: I need money, Tess. And I need a place to live. Did you factor that in to your yearnings?

TESS: Do you not know house prices are astronomical? Rodge and Di's dump went for one-point-five with no car park and no ensuite.

CURTIS: It had an ensuite.

TESS: No it didn't. You had to go out of the bedroom and into the hallway and then into the bathroom.

CURTIS: You didn't go into the hallway!

TESS: Yes, you did, Curtis.

CURTIS: Half a metre, there was the bathroom door. It was virtually an ensuite—

TESS: A 'virtual' ensuite is just a bathroom.

CURTIS: It doesn't have to be the inner city!

TESS: She's still at school!

CURTIS: Okay, one more year. If we sell at the same time we buy, it all evens out. Then we both rent and buy something smaller further out when she graduates.

TESS: I don't want to go 'further out'!

CURTIS: Well, Tess, we don't always get what we want.

TESS: Are you mad? You think we're going to buy anything for half what this costs?

CURTIS: You're such a princess. There are perfectly fine places you could afford.

TESS: I'm not living next to a McDonald's franchise so you are free to put your penis into tall short film-makers! Why should I? I had your child! I've been a reasonable mother! I've earned real money and kept a tidy linen cupboard! I've provided us with friends! I populate our world!

CURTIS: I make better than friends, Tess, I make lovers! You cosy up with your yearnings—I act on them! And I don't like the friends you made us! I hate your friends. They bore me to death.

TESS: You don't like my friends?

CURTIS: I like people who make a difference! I like people who help autistic kids at school for twenty bucks an hour and go home to watch 'Strictly Come Dancing' because they need a break from how shitty life is.

TESS: Is that really what you think of me? As someone who doesn't appreciate good people?

CURTIS: I don't *appreciate* them, Tess. I *like* them. I don't want to listen to conversations about where to buy preserved lemons!

TESS: That was one conversation!

CURTIS: The truth is, for you friendship is aspirational. That's why you liked Bonnie. You were impressed she owned an art gallery and you could hang out with women dressed like holocaust museums!

TESS, *about to respond, suddenly stops. All guile and bitterness appear to be suspended. Suddenly overwhelmed:*

TESS: This is awful.

CURTIS *feels it equally.*

CURTIS: It's really awful.

Beat.

They look at each other in mutual horror.

TESS: How can we do this to each other?

CURTIS: [*soft, reassuring them both*] People survive this.

TESS: All these years. We put so much effort into avoiding disaster. Not letting her sleep on her stomach, watching around pools, no flying over the Ukraine … I mean … we were experts at precipitating catastrophe. And look. Look at us. We've invited it to the table. Please come in … make yourself at home …

CURTIS: We make pointless decisions in the blind hope that we chart our own course. But then the weather sets in. And we just have to get through it. And you and I got through it. More or less.

They look at each other—a moment of recognition of all they have shared: years of common memories.

TESS: Remember when you woke me up at four a.m.? She was asleep in the cot at the end of the bed and I said: Why'd you wake me up? And you said: Tessie, Look at it. We made a human!

They look at each other—a shattering moment of unspeakable joy and loss.

Then the night we came back from Patti Smith. That awful Swiss babysitter—the one we thought might put her in a microwave—said: She walked! And you opened the prosecco and we drank it with Heidi and found out she'd been an Olympic figure skater and was actually really fun.

A powerful, transcendent intimacy has just snuck up on them. They look at each other for a moment from inside the memory.

They spontaneously come in close. TESS *puts her arms around him.* CURTIS *suddenly embraces her: feels her—the beginning of a sexual encounter—both charged with desire.*

TESS *quietly speaks as they continue to touch.*

This is where we brought her home. We can't sell this, Curtis. We have to keep it.

CURTIS *recoils, bitter, furious.*

Beat.

CURTIS: [*disgusted, embarrassed*] You mean *you* have to keep it. I can't believe you just did that! I can't believe you used our history as collateral—

TESS: [*genuine, traumatised*] I loved you! I loved you! I loved you! I love you! I love you, Curtis! I love you!

CURTIS: [*tough*] I don't care.

TESS: [*hurt and suddenly angry*] Where is your pride? Where is your decency? I'm the mother! The mother gets the house! Do you really want our daughter to spend three hours a day on public transport? I'm not moving, Curtis. I'm keeping the house! I bought it! I bought it!

CURTIS: It wasn't just you!

TESS: Mum and Dad paid the deposit, as well you remember. *My* mother and father, not yours. And I paid most of the mortgage and most of the bills!

CURTIS: I paid for the bathroom with the tutoring money!

TESS: Only the hardware! I paid for the labour!

CURTIS: I paid the tiler! I remember!

TESS: Fifteen years ago? You remember paying the tiler?

CURTIS: I remember paying the tiler!

TESS: Probably memorable because it was the one time you paid for something! I paid for the floors! I paid for the garden!

CURTIS: *I* paid for the garage door!

TESS: I paid for the garage door!

CURTIS: No—no—no—no—I paid for the garage door! Remember I had the Bunnings voucher?

TESS: I paid for nearly everything and well you know it!

CURTIS: Because editing pays better than teaching. Not because you're a better person. Not because you're smarter. Not because you work harder.

TESS: Don't blame me that you suddenly realise what it costs. What life costs.

CURTIS: I know what life costs!

TESS: I don't think you do! That's the problem with moving on from your financially solvent wife … You can't use *her* money to finance *your* lover.

CURTIS: You moved on first.

An impasse. Beat.

CURTIS, *unable to bear it, tries Mr Nice Guy.*

Tess … Tess … you're right. Of course we have to safeguard what is precious, what is—

Brutal, hard as nails, she interrupts:

TESS: I'll give you a hundred grand to go away.

Silent shock at the bluntness of this.

Long beat.

CURTIS: [*quietly*] Is this what we've come to?

TESS: [*hard, practical*] Almost everyone comes to this. It's a fair offer. You can walk away and put a deposit on something.

CURTIS: Everything you have ever had has been given to you … every connection, every piece of luck. Handed to you. And you're never grateful. You're not entitled to happiness. It is a myth that destroys our perfectly good lives by insisting we believe in it.

TESS: I believe in happiness. I have to.

CURTIS: No-one owes you, Tess.

TESS: And no-one can fix you, Curtis. No-one can fix your lifelong feelings of being underqualified and unexceptional. No-one can fix those things but you. You became a teacher because you knew you couldn't impress adults. Which is why you're with Greta right now because when push comes to shove you just can't cut it with a grown-up woman.

CURTIS: You cunt!

TESS: Any real woman would see through you in a minute: a talented, nice-looking school teacher and nothing more. Not Mr Fucking Chips! And deep down you know you took the easy road to self-worth and it gnaws at you. It gnaws at you and all the more when you look at the people in my life who have ideas. Because they take a gamble on themselves. They take a big fat gamble on themselves and you never gambled a thing. You want their courage. You want their self-belief. You want their freedom. But you're never going to have it, because you're scared.

CURTIS: I am scared. But as luck would have it, I like the high seas of new romance. It's strange and rough and confronting, but it's exciting.

Beat.

I'll take the hundred grand.

SCENE FIFTEEN

Curtis and Tess's house. CURTIS, TESS, BONNIE, ANNIE.

BONNIE *and* ANNIE *watch as* CURTIS *and* TESS *hold up objects.* CURTIS *places things in his box.* TESS, *by contrast, is not putting anything in her box.*

CURTIS *holds up the 'No Secrets' album by Carly Simon.*

TESS: My sister gave it to me with 'After the Goldrush'. I know every word to those albums.

CURTIS: Actually, it's my copy.

TESS *stops. Looks at him. Looks down at it.*

TESS: Curtis, you didn't like Carly Simon. You said her mouth was too big.

CURTIS: You raved about it on our first date, so I bought it. Your copy is mixed up with the Joni's.

TESS *walks over to* CURTIS *and hands him the album. As he takes it, she holds onto it so there is a little awkward push and pull. He stops pulling and, hand still on it, looks at* TESS. *She stares back and lets it go.*

ANNIE *starts rifling through the Joni Mitchell albums, pulls out another 'No Secrets' and hands it to* TESS *who puts this one in her box.*

I'm assuming you want the feminist stuff … *Second Sex* … *Beauty Myth* …?

TESS: I think you need them more than me.

BONNIE: Good call.

CURTIS: [*to* BONNIE] Why don't you keep quiet? [*Back to* TESS] Most of the travel guides are out of date. But some have annotations, so?

TESS: Bin them.

CURTIS *looks at them, suddenly sad.*

CURTIS: I might keep the *Time Out Paris* from '96 … What about the folios we got from Noel and Dinah as a wedding present? I think there are twenty-three, if I'm correct … which I think I am … so we could take eleven each and whoever gets the *Greek Myths* gets two volumes?

TESS: Oh, good plan, Curtis!

CURTIS: Which eleven?

TESS: You choose.

CURTIS: Shouldn't we go one by one?
TESS: No.
CURTIS: Well, I feel bad doing that.

Irritated, he puts an armful of books in his box and, determined, places a pile of books in a pile for TESS.

With the art books, I assume we alternate. Unless we want to do movements.
TESS: Movements?
CURTIS: You take Abstract Expressionism and I take, ah, Photography.
TESS: Oh, that's brilliant. That's a brilliant idea. Movements.

CURTIS *looks at her: Is she taking the piss?*

CURTIS: Tess …

ANNIE *picks up a book and looks at the title.*

ANNIE: *Tropical Rainforests*.

Reflexively, TESS *starts a funereal tap routine.*

CURTIS: [*to* TESS] Will you shut the fuck up?

TESS *comes to a halt.*

CURTIS, BONNIE *and* ANNIE *turn back to the books. With dignity,* CURTIS *regards three books he lifts from the shelf.*

We have three *Mayors of Casterbridge.*
TESS: Three *Mayor of Casterbridges.*
CURTIS: [*irritated*] Okay, Tess. Okay. Fine.
TESS: You take 'em.
CURTIS: [*frustrated*] Tess, I don't need three copies. Can you—ah—would it be possible for you to co-operate?
TESS: Curtis, I'm saying: Take everything. It's hard to think of a more co-operative attitude.
ANNIE: Exactly.
CURTIS: [*to* ANNIE] I thought you were on my side?
ANNIE: You just got happy so fast, Curtis!
BONNIE: It's disgusting, Curtis!
CURTIS: How long did you want me to suffer for? Come on! Put a number on it!
BONNIE: Did you even have one night of existential panic?

ANNIE: That means wrestling with the big questions—
CURTIS: I know what 'existential' means, Annie!
TESS: Take the Hardys, Curtis.
CURTIS: You know exactly what you're doing!

CURTIS *and* TESS *lock eyes—a moment of confirmation.*

Beat.

[*Utterly frustrated, but soldiering on*] Okay … the D. H. Lawrence first edition Penguins. I actually found them on Gumtree.
TESS: [*ironic*] It was my PayPal account but you pressed 'Confirm and Pay', so where does that leave us?
CURTIS: Tess. I'm hoping we can be civilised.
TESS: You don't want to 'drag this out'. Let's just do it and get on with our lives.
CURTIS: That's exactly it. Yes.
TESS: Are people who stay, stronger than people who leave? Is it braver to fight or to cut your losses?

CURTIS *stares at her. Why is she raising this profoundly disturbing question now? They hold each other's gaze for a moment and then* TESS *backs down.*

She picks up a baby names book and holds it in the air.

You can have the baby names book … Obvious reasons.
CURTIS: Tess—
TESS: Take the books, Curtis!
CURTIS: No, I won't!
TESS: I don't want them!
CURTIS: Yes, you do!

TESS *throws* CURTIS *the baby names book and he reflexively catches it.*

Meanwhile, ANNIE, *horrified, is trying to escape by combing the shelves.*

TESS: You always liked 'Winston' and I said over my dead body. So this way, you might get your Winston and I won't have to die!
CURTIS: I'm getting mad, Tess.
BONNIE: Look, you two need to decide how to respond to each other.
TESS: You don't 'decide' how to respond, Bonnie.

BONNIE: Of course you do. Everything's a choice.

TESS: We didn't choose to do this!

BONNIE: It's a choice to leave or stay. Every morning it's a choice. Love is a decision!

TESS: What?

CURTIS: Are you mad?

ANNIE *turns to look at* BONNIE, *shocked.*

BONNIE: Love doesn't just erupt out of the wilderness. It's not emotional! You decide when to stop looking.

CURTIS: You didn't fall in love with Annie?

BONNIE: I decided to. It's the same thing.

ANNIE: [*confused*] But, Bonnie …

BONNIE: You just don't understand—

ANNIE: [*her anger rising*] I don't understand! The truth is you don't like anyone to contradict you!

CURTIS: Oh, *touché*!

BONNIE: I'd love it if someone could prove me wrong once in a while!

ANNIE: 'Someone'?

TESS: You can't stand to think you're not in control, Bonnie. Have you noticed that?

BONNIE: I can't stand sentimental rubbish, Tess. That's what I can't stand.

TESS: We fell! And he fell out! It's a slow-motion fall.

BONNIE: He gave himself permission to flirt!

TESS: It's not immoral to flirt!

ANNIE: Tess, if you love someone, you don't flirt!

TESS: *You* flirt, Annie!

Beat.

BONNIE: She doesn't flirt!

ANNIE: I don't flirt!

TESS: You do flirt! You're a big flirt!

BONNIE: I think I'd know if Annie was a flirt!

ANNIE: Who do I flirt with?

TESS: Me.

BONNIE: What?

TESS: The Kakadu trip!

BONNIE: What about the Kakadu trip?

CURTIS: What happened on the Kakadu trip?

TESS: [*to* ANNIE] You flirted with me the entire trip!

CURTIS and BONNIE: [*simultaneously*] What?

ANNIE: That's not—

TESS: You said we should shower together!

ANNIE: To save water!

Over the next section, TESS *collects a huge armful of the books* CURTIS *has placed in a pile for her.*

CURTIS: [*to* ANNIE] So you're allowed to flirt, but I'm not?

BONNIE: Well, this is just fantastic!

ANNIE: [*to* TESS] You propositioned me at the truck stop!

TESS: Only because you said I should try it!

ANNIE: You said you wanted a lesbian experience by the time you were thirty! I was just trying to help you out!

TESS: Well, nothing happened!

ANNIE: Exactly! Nothing happened!

TESS: Because I was in love with Curtis!

ANNIE: Because I was in love with Bonnie! [*She can't resist making the point.*] And because ... in the end ... you were too conventional.

TESS: Too conventional?

CURTIS: Listen, sorry, but you two are much more conventional than us. Bonnie is the patriarch and you're the little wifey-wifey.

BONNIE: My God!

ANNIE: 'Wifey wifey'?

CURTIS: In straight marriages, there's usually one woman and one metrosexual. With you guys, there's always the big woman and the little woman. I'm just saying—

BONNIE: My God!

CURTIS: Annie is the acolyte. She's there to make you feel powerful and important.

ANNIE: I'm not there for anything.

BONNIE: [*to* CURTIS] That's really offensive.

CURTIS: [*to* BONNIE] Why do you insist she traipse around after you at openings holding your pinot while you talk about the biomorphic diversity of the primal form.

BONNIE *stares at* CURTIS. *Unforgiveable.*

The moment breaks with a crash as TESS *dumps the armful of books in* CURTIS*'s box, spilling onto the floor.*

TESS: You can have everything. All of it. You can take it all.

She walks across the floor and takes the tantalus off the shelf. She holds it and looks at him.

Beat.

Everything except the tantalus.

CURTIS: You only want the tantalus?

TESS: Yes.

She sets the tantalus down on the floor in the middle of the room.

CURTIS: Tess … Tess … it's my tantalus.

From the shelf, ANNIE *has pulled out the battered copy of* Tender is the Night.

ANNIE: [*crestfallen*] *Tender is the Night*.

In silence, they all acknowledge the importance of this find. CURTIS *looks stricken, then mans up.*

CURTIS: Flip for it.

TESS: [*sadly*] I fell for you over that book.

CURTIS *mistakenly registers this as an act of truce.*

CURTIS: Tess …

TESS: But the whole thing was a lie. If only I'd seen through it, maybe this entire chain of events would never have unfolded.

This is really painful to CURTIS.

I'll trade you. You have everything in the house and the Fitzgerald … but leave me the tantalus.

Long beat.

CURTIS *is thinking about it—tension. Then finally:*

CURTIS: No.

Beat.

TESS*'s expression starts to contort into utter rage.*

BONNIE: Tess—

ANNIE: Tess, look—

TESS *throws herself at* CURTIS, *completely out of control, attacking him with her fists.*

TESS: You mean, fucking bastard! Fuck fuck fuck fuck you you you you Why? Why? What did I—? Why? Why? What happened? What—what—what—Curtis! You loved me. We made her.

She hits him hard—it hurts. He hits TESS *reflexively and she falls to the floor, her head crunching. Books go flying. Screams. Everything stops. No- one moves.*

Suddenly, TESS *rises from the dead and violently launches herself at* CURTIS. *Panic. Screams.* BONNIE *and* ANNIE *run over to them.* TESS *and* CURTIS *are struggling—it's raw and real and savage. They're inflicting real blows.*

ANNIE *struggles to pull* TESS *off* CURTIS.

ANNIE: [*to* TESS] Get off him!

BONNIE *launches herself at* ANNIE *in retaliation, on* TESS*'s behalf, and* ANNIE *flies back, pulling herself up and landing a punch on* BONNIE, *who slaps* ANNIE *across the face while* CURTIS *and* TESS *are trying to kill each other.*

In the midst of the melee, ANNIE *suddenly screams:*

Flat battery! Flat battery! Flat battery!

CURTIS *and* TESS *are still struggling with each other while* BONNIE, *alerted by* ANNIE*'s screaming, stops.*

ANNIE *and* BONNIE *absorb what they are doing to each other, shocked.*

They are a tableau of still, spent, weary despair in contrast to the ungainly tussling of CURTIS *and* TESS, *who continue to wrestle around on the floor.*

As TESS *picks up a lethal-looking stool to break over* CURTIS*'s head, the moment between* BONNIE *and* ANNIE *breaks and* BONNIE *tries to pull* CURTIS *away while* ANNIE *grabs the stool from* TESS.

BONNIE: Call the cops!
ANNIE: [*to* TESS] You'll kill him!
BONNIE: [*struggling*] Don't fucking touch her, Curtis!
TESS: [*to* ANNIE, *struggling*] Get off me!

They fight to free themselves from BONNIE *and* ANNIE*'s grip.*

CURTIS: Let go! Fuck off, Bonnie!

CURTIS *and* TESS *are trying to kill each other and undo the grip of their friends.* TESS *lunges at* CURTIS.

ANNIE: [*pulling at her*] You're crazy!

CURTIS *tries to push* TESS *away.*

BONNIE: I'm going to fucking kill you, Curtis!
TESS: Leave him alone!
ANNIE: Shut up, Tess!
TESS: Get off him!

CURTIS *pushes* BONNIE *away and stands up.* TESS *extricates herself from* ANNIE*'s grip.*

All four are standing still, trying to absorb what has just happened. All four are war-torn—bloodied, hair astray, clothes mussed, faces red, in pain.

[*To* BONNIE *and* ANNIE] You don't need to be here. [*To* CURTIS] They don't need to be here.

CURTIS: We don't need you.
ANNIE: You wanted us to be here!
BONNIE: You asked us to come!
CURTIS: You're always around!
ANNIE: You want us around!
BONNIE: You need us around!
ANNIE: We wanted to help!
CURTIS: But you don't help! You're no help!
TESS: You're not us!
CURTIS: You're not us!
TESS: You're nothing like us!
CURTIS: You're two completely other people!
TESS: Okay, you are like us but you're not us!
CURTIS: You can't possibly understand!

ANNIE: What does that mean?

TESS: You're two beautiful people and I love you, but you can't understand! You just can't understand!

CURTIS: You should go!

BONNIE: So you can hit her again?

ANNIE: Shut up, Bonnie!

BONNIE: I'm looking after her!

CURTIS: She doesn't want you to!

TESS: I don't want you to!

ANNIE: Why couldn't we understand?

CURTIS: Because this is our story.

A moment of silence as they absorb the meaning of this.

[*Gently, but very sure*] The thing is, Annie—Bonnie—the thing is—

TESS: You see—

CURTIS: I think Tess and I—have a bit of a yearning to … to separate from you.

Silence as BONNIE *and* ANNIE *contemplate this with shock.*

Calmly, ANNIE *walks over to the tantalus.*

BONNIE: Annie …

ANNIE *picks it up.*

Annie …

Without any fanfare, ANNIE *drops it. As it smashes onto the ground, one of the two crystal decanters smashes.*

A long, long beat as all four take in the splintered remains of the tantalus.

ANNIE: When I first met you, Curtis, I couldn't believe how big your thoughts were. All your ideas about transforming the world. I thought … Why is it that I've never thought about that stuff? And then when you got together with Tess and then I met Bonnie … all three of you were so in love with your potential. It never occurred to me that I could make a difference. I thought: What's wrong with me? My parents never encouraged such thoughts. It was just … How will you fill your days? How will you make money to pay the car registration? I felt so … poor … Now that I see you … clearly …

Now I realise … your yearnings … the way you wield words … it's all a distraction … You'll never be free of a sense of failure. Because it's really all about … kindness. Nothing grand. Nothing earth shattering. And you and Tess … you can keep struggling for answers but sometimes they're … unattainable. The choice is just to be … in the moment—kind. And you're right. It is your story. It's your fucking story. It's not our story. [*To* BONNIE, *imperiously*] Get your stuff.

BONNIE; We can't leave them!

ANNIE: [*fearlessly commanding*] Get in the fucking car, Bonnie.

BONNIE, *intimidated by* ANNIE*'s newly commanding persona, timidly runs to collect her things.*

They walk to the door, watched on by TESS *and* CURTIS.

The solemnity of the moment is interrupted by the insistent knocking at the door. All four stand still, confused.

More urgent knocking.

BONNIE, *nearest the door, crawls to it and peeks through the viewfinder.*

BONNIE: [*whispering to the others*] It's Greta!

All four, panicked, immediately bob down. United terror at Greta's presence. Fast whispering between them:

TESS: [*appalled, to* CURTIS] She's been waiting out there?

CURTIS: [*to* TESS] You said it would be quick!

TESS: [*to* CURTIS] Because I didn't want anything! You started insisting!

BONNIE: [*to* CURTIS] That was sensitive. Bringing her.

CURTIS: [*to* BONNIE] I didn't 'bring her'. She got in the car!

ANNIE: [*to* CURTIS] That's 'bringing her', Curtis!

BONNIE: [*to* CURTIS] You're dividing the relics of a marriage and you bring the new recruit. Tacky!

TESS *suddenly stands, walks across the room, picks up the copy of* Tender is the Night *and walks towards the door, watched with awe and suspense by the other three.*

CURTIS *suddenly follows her, aware of what she is about to do.*

CURTIS: No, Tess! No!

TESS *opens the door and passes the book to the unseen Greta, whom she addresses:*

TESS: I want you to have it.

BONNIE: Oh, Jesus!

CURTIS: [*yelling hysterically at the unseen Greta*] Don't take it! Don't take it!

The book suddenly flies through the air, chucked at CURTIS *by the unseen Greta.* CURTIS *is hit in the head by it.* TESS *slams the door shut.*

The book falls to the floor, pulsing with significance as they stare at it.

A car door slams and then the relentless sound of a hand on the horn blasts through the house.

BONNIE *and* ANNIE *straighten themselves up and stiffly stand by the door.*

ANNIE: Goodbye, Tess. 'Bye, Curtis.

TESS: Thank you for coming.

CURTIS: Thanks. For everything.

A long beat as TESS *and* CURTIS *watch on as* ANNIE *and* BONNIE *exit. They close the door behind them.* CURTIS *and* TESS *are finally alone.*

CURTIS *rescues the one decanter to survive from the shards of glass and wood of the tantalus. He pours two drinks as the horn finally comes to a stop.*

He walks over to TESS, *hands her one of the Scotches he has poured and stands opposite her. They take each other in.*

Hey.

Beat.

TESS: Hey.

They both take a slug of their drink.

A rapid-fire knock on the front door, followed by momentary pounding.

TESS *and* CURTIS *continue to stare at each other, drinking each other in.*

The banging starts again, moving into an amplified reverberating sound.

It continues as the lights fade to black.

THE END